THE SENATE INSTITUTION

THE SENATE INSTITUTION

Edited by
NATHANIEL STONE PRESTON
The American University

NEW PERSPECTIVES
IN
POLITICAL SCIENCE

VAN NOSTRAND REINHOLD COMPANY
NEW YORK   CINCINNATI   TORONTO
LONDON   MELBOURNE

Van Nostrand Reinhold Company Regional Offices:
Cincinnati, New York, Chicago, Millbrae, Dallas

Van Nostrand Reinhold Company Foreign Offices:
London, Toronto, Melbourne

Copyright © 1969 by LITTON EDUCATIONAL PUBLISHING, INC.

All rights reserved. No part of this work covered by the copyrights hereon may be reproduced or used in any form or by any means—graphic, electronic, or mechanical, including photocopying, recording, taping, or information storage and retrieval systems—without written permission of the publisher. Manufactured in the United States of America.

Published by Van Nostrand Reinhold Company
450 West 33rd Street, New York, N. Y. 10001

Published simultaneously in Canada by
D. Van Nostrand Company (Canada), Ltd.
15 14 13 12 11 10 9 8 7 6 5 4 3 2 1

To
ROBERT J. WICHSER

Preface

IN THE SPRING OF 1965, A NUMBER OF UNITED STATES SENATORS TOOK part in an unusual educational experiment at The American University in Washington, D.C. Appearing as guest lecturers in a course entitled "The Senate Institution" given by the editor of this volume, they described in their own way the workings of the unique legislative body of which they are members.

Ten of these lectures, revised into essay form and brought up to date by their authors in the spring of 1967, constitute the heart of the present work. To them has been added an entirely new essay which the Assistant Minority Leader, the Honorable Thomas H. Kuchel, was kind enough to write to describe an important aspect of the Senate's organization. Also published for the first time is the addendum which the Honorable Mike Mansfield, Majority Leader of the Senate, has written to accompany his 1963 Statement in defense of his leadership.

Most of the original lectures were delivered extemporaneously or from sketchy notes, and the revision and editing has not erased entirely the evidences of oral discourse. One hopes that the reader will agree that this is fitting. The Senate transacts its business orally for the most part. Much as a bureaucracy subsists on memoranda, the Senate lives on and through its speeches and its colloquies. It is a living Senate that we are trying to present here.

To the senators and their staffs who gave so freely of their time both to the original lectures and to the tiresome business of revision, to Senators Kuchel and Mansfield for their helpful contributions to the present work, and to Vice President Hubert H. Humphrey for permission to use his commencement speech at Syracuse University, the editor here records his thanks.

Gratitude is also owed to the editors of the New Perspective Series, Professor William G. Andrews of the State University College at Brockport, N.Y., and Professor Franklin L. Burdette of the University of Maryland, and to Messrs. Baxter Venable and Gardner M. Spungin at Van Nostrand Reinhold Company for their most useful criticism and suggestions; to Provost Harold H. Hutson and The American University for the release of the University's rights to the lecture series; and to Mrs. Marjorie M. Moomey for her usual flawless typing.

This book is dedicated to a student, Robert J. Wichser, to honor not only him, but all students who seek their own education actively. He was a prime mover in urging The American University to present the course in which these lectures were delivered and, with the aid and encouragement of the Associate Dean of the School of Government and Public Administration, Dr. Charles H. Goodman, worked tirelessly in arranging for the participation of the senators in it.

N.S.P.
Washington, D.C.

Contents

PREFACE ... vii

THE SENATE IN THE AMERICAN SYSTEM

I   A TRIBUTE TO THE CONGRESS
    by Vice President Hubert H. Humphrey ... 3

II THE SENATE AS ENVISIONED BY THE FRAMERS OF THE CONSTITUTION
    by Senator Wayne L. Morse ... 7

III THE ROLE OF EXECUTIVE LEADERSHIP
    by Senator Gale W. McGee ... 18

IV THE ROLE OF THE SENATE IN DETERMINING FOREIGN POLICY
    by Senator John J. Sparkman ... 31

THE SENATOR AS POLITICIAN

V   SENATORIAL CAMPAIGNING
    by Senator Thruston B. Morton ... 43

VI THE RELATIONSHIP OF A SENATOR TO HIS CONSTITUENCY
    by Senator Hugh Scott ... 50

THE LEADERSHIP AND THE PARTIES

VII THE SENATE AND ITS LEADERSHIP
     by Senator Michael J. Mansfield ... 59

VIII THE ROLE OF THE SENATE MINORITY
     by Senator Thomas H. Kuchel ... 75

ON THE SENATE FLOOR

IX THE DEBATE ON SENATE RULES CHANGE, 1959 ... 85

"WHERE THE WORK IS DONE"

X COMMITTEES AND SUBCOMMITTEES IN THE SENATE
   by Senator Edmund S. Muskie — 121

XI THE ROLE OF COMMITTEE INVESTIGATIONS
   by Senator Karl E. Mundt — 132

THE PROBLEM OF ETHICS

XII CONGRESSIONAL ETHICS
   by Senator Eugene J. McCarthy — 147

XIII THE DODD CENSURE RESOLUTION DEBATE — 159

REFORM AND THE FUTURE OF THE SENATE

XIV THE CASE FOR CONGRESSIONAL REFORM
   by Senator Joseph S. Clark — 175

XV THE CASE AGAINST REFORM: A NOBLER PURPOSE THAN POLITICAL EFFICIENCY
   by Senator Sam J. Ervin, Jr. — 192

THE SENATE INSTITUTION

The Senate in the American System

The Senate is the great curiosity of the American political system. Alone among the so-called upper houses of the world, it enjoys great power—greater than that of its popular opposite chamber. It holds an absolute veto over legislation and the power to deny the most powerful of freely-elected executives his choice of men to fill the posts of his administration. It can, and once did, keep this country from taking a leading place in the family of nations. Unrepresentative, sometimes arrogant, and proudly holding to procedures no other legislative body still maintains, it yet remains an integral part of the governmental structure of a nation which proclaims itself to be democratic.

Central to an understanding of the Senate is the point made by Senator Sparkman in the fourth of the selections which follow: That its power is essentially negative. It is not a power to achieve in and of itself, but to deny. And this is characteristic of American Constitutional arrangements generally. The uniqueness of the Senate within the American system lies in the fact that, by its lack of rules for limiting debate, for preventing procedural delays, and (saving three hours each day) for requiring germaneness, it confers its negative power liberally upon its members. A handful of senators, or even one, can keep the Senate from acting at a critical moment and thus exact concessions or, at the very least, a hearing for the interest he or they represent. The Senate is, therefore, the extreme expression of the American Constitutional principle.

The four selections which open this book deal with the Senate in relation to the system of which it is a part.

Vice President Humphrey, in paying tribute to the Congress, does not specify the Senate. Yet we may be forgiven, perhaps, for suspecting that he has in mind the body in which he served for sixteen years and over which he then presided. He makes explicit for us the rationale behind the negative powers with which we have endowed our legislative branch: The checks exist to compel compromise and moderation. In a nation of great diversity, according to Mr. Humphrey, the ac-

commodation of conflicting views is an essential factor distinguishing democracy from tryanny.

The remaining three essays converge on one central theme: the preoccupation of the Senate with its historic role in foreign affairs. In his consideration of the present functions of the Senate in the light of its history, Senator Morse gravitates inevitably to the issue of its declining power over foreign policy, while Senator McGee finds himself faced with the same issue in observing the relations of the Senate with the Executive. In so doing he takes issue with his colleague. It remains, finally, for Senator Sparkman to describe the role as it is performed today.

I. A Tribute to the Congress*

Vice President Hubert H. Humphrey

... I WANT TO DISCUSS ... THE IMPORTANCE OF ONE OF THE great Constitutional instruments at the disposal of the American people in the business of making democracy work. I refer to the institution of the United States Congress. What I have to say, I think, needs saying because all too many of our citizens take an indifferent, or even a hostile, view toward the legislative branch. This is not to underestimate the need for strong and able Presidential leadership or for wise and humane judicial decisions. It is, however, to reaffirm the vital role of Congress in our Constitutional system.

Few persons can deal directly with either a President or a Supreme Court. But any person can communicate with his elected representatives in Washington. The members of Congress provide a direct link between the national government and the almost 195 million persons who compromise this Republic. Surely this connection is vital in keeping our national government responsive to the needs and opinions of the American people.

I have found Congressional service to be a remarkable form of higher education. My teachers have been Presidents and department heads, constituents and the press and, above all, a group of wise and distinguished colleagues in both houses. I cannot ... convey to you all that I have learned from these teachers. But perhaps I can suggest some lessons in democratic theory and practice which I have gained from my collegial experiences in Congress.

The first lesson has to do with the creative and constructive dimension to the process of compromise.

* Address at Syracuse University, Syracuse, New York, June 6, 1965. The title has been supplied by the editor.

There are 100 members of the United States Senate; 435 members of the House. They come from states and districts as diverse as Nevada and New York, Alaska and Alabama. No two states or regions of the United States have identical interests or prejudices. One of the jobs of Congress is to reconcile such differences through the process of compromise and accommodation. What sometimes seem to the untutored eye to be legislative obstructionisms are often no more than the honest expressions of dedicated representatives—trying to make clear the attitudes and interests of their states and regions.

As Sir Richard Grenfell once observed: "Mankind is slowly learning that because two men differ neither need be wicked." From the earliest days of this Republic—at the Constitutional Convention of 1787—the leaders of this nation have maintained an unwavering commitment to moderation. If our founding fathers had not understood the need to overcome extremes in drafting our Constitution, this noble experiment in the art of self-government would have surely foundered on the rocks of dissension and discord. As in the deliberations of the Constitutional Convention, the heart of Congressional activity are skills of negotiation—of honest bargaining among equals. My willingness to compromise—and I have done so more times than I can count—is the respect I pay to the dignity of those with whom I disagree. Through reasonable discussion, through taking into account the views of many, Congress amends and refines legislative proposals so that once a law is passed it reflects the collective judgment of a diverse people.

Surely this is a remarkable service. Surely, the habits of accommodation and compromise are of universal consequence. These are the skills and attitudes so desperately needed on the larger stage of world conflict. World order and the rule of law will be secure on this earth only when men have learned to cope with the continuing conflicts of peoples and nations through peaceful processes of legislative bargaining.

A second lesson I have learned from my Congressional teachers is the importance of the Congressional role of responsible surveillance. There are roughly 70 separate departments and agencies of the Federal government. Some are small; some are large. All are engaged in carrying out the will of the people as expressed through Congress. In the interests of efficiency, economy, and responsiveness, these departments and agencies need a continuing critical review by the committees and Houses of Congress. The genius of our founding fathers is nowhere more in evidence than in those sections of the Constitution which provide for checks and balances. Through its review of the executive budget in the appropriations process, through committee investigations, through advice and consent on appointments and treaties, and through informal discussion, Congress seeks to improve and to support the executive branch of the government.

This exercise in freedom protects and extends freedom. If legislative voices are occasionally strident, citizens should take stock of what their world would be like if no legislative voices were heard at all. We know what happens in countries without independent and constructively analytical legislatures. Mankind invented a word for such systems centuries ago. The word is "tyranny."

But there is a final lesson I have learned from my Congressional teachers: the creative joy of politics. Each Congress is devoted in substantial measure to the development of new public policies designed to promote the general welfare and the national security of this nation. Congress is not a battlefield for blind armies that clash by night. It is a place where national objectives are sought—where Presidential programs are reviewed—where great societies are endlessly debated and implemented.

If, as Emerson once wrote, Congress is a "standing insurrection," it is a standing insurrection against the ancient enemies of mankind: war, poverty, ignorance, injustice, sickness, environmental ugliness, economic and personal insecurity.

Few careers open such remarkable opportunities for translating dreams into reality. A new bill, a creative amendment, a wise appropriation, may mean the difference between health and sickness, jobs and idleness, peace and war for millions of human beings. Stemming from ancient parliamentary origins, the main job of Congress is to redress grievances, to right wrongs, to make freedom and justice living realities for all. What higher calling exists? This is the essence of politics: to translate the concerns and the creative responses of a vast citizenry into effective and humane laws.

I cannot conclude without a personal note. For almost 20 years, Congress has been my home. As Vice President, my relationships with my former colleagues are inevitably more formal and more intermittent than in past years. Yet I can say unashamedly that I cherish them dearly. I have seen their weaknesses as they have seen mine. I have on occasion been restive of delays and procedural anachronisms—and so have they. But I have seen in the Halls of Congress more idealism, more humaneness and compassion, more empathy, more understanding, more profiles of courage than in any other institution I have ever known. Like many of you today, I find it in my heart to praise and to thank my teachers.

Perhaps some of these brief words of tribute to the institution of freedom known as the U.S. Congress may stay with you. As long as Congress continues to function as a responsible and viable element in our Constitutional system, the promise of American democracy will forever endure—the torch of freedom will forever light the path of the future....

II. The Senate as Envisioned by the Framers of the Constitution

Senator Wayne L. Morse*

AMONG THE OTHER CURIOSITIES OF HISTORIOGRAPHY IN THIS country, surely the shift in the reputations of the men who hammered out a Constitution in Philadelphia in 1787 must rank among the most curious. For many generations, a myth was nurtured that those men of bone and blood like ourselves were in reality nothing less than demigods. Their eyes were constantly on the stars, devotedly following those basic principles of good government to which there could be no refutation. And into the golden goblet of the Constitution they poured to the very brim that ineluctable wisdom which no one in his right mind, or at least only ignorant foreigners, could deny.

As was to be expected, the pendulum eventually swung to the other extreme. The glorious patriots, under the new lenses ground by men like Charles A. Beard, were now revealed—or perhaps reviled—as selfish, self-seeking capitalists devoted to preserving the interests of their economic class. It was discovered and "proved" that the Founding Fathers were simply another example of mechanistic economic determinism, their eyes not on the stars but on the dollar.

Both of these extreme views have been discredited among men of sense in our own day. Most historians of our generation look upon the delegates to that momentous Constitutional Convention as familiar human beings, men who had ambitions and ideals,

* Senator Morse wishes it stated that he is indebted to the Library of Congress for much of the historical background of the Constitutional Convention and early history of the Senate presented in this essay.

families and foibles, private interests and public goals. Aside from the difference in numbers, and taking into account the differences in education, they could easily be mistaken in these regards for one of our better modern congresses.

Is that too heretical a statement? I think not. We are all too prone to underestimate our own generation and to overestimate the wisdom of the generations we know only through the filtering curtain of history.

If this view of those men in Philadelphia is essentially correct, then certain other misconceptions about what they accomplished in that place and in that time must fall along with the ones I have already mentioned. One of these is that the Constitution-writers held a clear and unanimous view of what they had brought forth and particularly of this unique and curious institution they devised and named the Senate. To approach the Constitution and the governmental structure provided in it from that narrow perspective is to misconceive completely the true quality of the Convention's accomplishments.

James Madison's voluminous notes on the proceedings of the Convention, the notes of other participants, and the correspondence of the delegates clearly indicate the wide variety of opinions and views these men had on the many subjects they discussed. Probably every delegate was dissatisfied with at least some major portion of the final draft.

This is not to say that there was no unity at all. On the contrary, by and large the Framers were generally agreed as to broad purpose and even as to some important details.

We know that they were in various degrees disenchanted with that "rope of sand," the Articles of Confederation. Not all of them; Yates and Lansing of New York and Martin of Maryland were almost interlopers at Philadelphia. But by and large the delegates shared at least this view.

Most, again in importantly differing degrees, agreed that some restraints had to be laid on the State governments. A large majority wanted some kind of powerful central government that would have the authority to legislate effectively on matters of national concern.

In the details of the matter they wanted the new government to have three departments—legislative, executive, and judicial—and they hoped to prevent the misuse of power by pitting these elements against each other, although even here some delegates, for example, Hamilton, disagreed.

We know, in short, that the delegates were mostly agreed on some important fundamentals. But in the degree to which they were devoted to these fundamentals there were vast and crucial differences. So when it came to devising the structure of the new government it was inevitable, if anything at all was to be accomplished, that the result would reflect not unanimity but the delicate and often untidy balance of a tug of war. In other words, many critical Constitutional provisions were arrived at by compromises, great and small and seemingly endless. Perhaps the comparison with a modern Congress appears less heretical at this point.

The second misconception that must fall is the one that attributes a theoretical symmetry to the government embodied in the Constitution. In one scholar's words, the Constitution was not "a victory for abstract theory. . . ." It was, instead, a victory for hard-headed political realism. It was not a blueprint for Utopia; almost every delegate's Utopia had been thoroughly riddled by one compromise or another. The writings of Locke and Montesquieu undoubtedly had their influence and showed up in various ways in the final document. But the practical details of the Constitution were, it seems to me, less based on theoretical propositions than on the exigencies of the moment.

REPRESENTATION OF THE STATES IN THE SENATE

Everything said about the character of the Constitution to this point applies with even more intensity to the Senate. The most bitter debate of the Convention revolved about the essential nature of that body, for it was in the composition of the Senate that the role of the States in the new system had to be determined. On the composition of the Senate, "disagreement," in Swanstrom's words, "was so violent that it threatened to break up the Convention. . . . Nearly all of the issues involving the powers and composition of Congress were vitally affected in one way or another by this great central issue."

This is no exaggeration. One hothead, Gunning Bedford of Delaware, threatened that if the small States did not have their way in that dispute they would find "some foreign ally, of more honor and good faith, who will take them by the hand, and do them justice." John Dickinson of the same State declared that "we would sooner submit to a foreign power than . . . be deprived of an equality of suffrage in both branches of the Legislature, and thereby be thrown under the domination of the large States." Gouverneur Morris, representing the large State of Pennsylvania, grimly replied that the country must be united. "If persuasion did not unite it, the sword would." Rufus King, speaking for another large State, Massachusetts, told the Convention he "preferred doing nothing rather than to allow an equal vote to all States."

Fortunately, tempers eventually cooled. What Madison characterized as a "chasm" was eventually bridged, in Haynes' metaphor, by "one of the most difficult engineering feats in the whole history of the Convention." The Great Compromise, as it came to be known, was little loved by anyone, but eventually supported by most—representation by population in the House and by States in the Senate.

In a quite candid passage in the Federalist No. 62, Hamilton said of it:

> The equality of representation in the Senate is another point, which, being evidently the result of compromise between the opposite pretensions of the large and the small states, does not call for much discussion. . . . It is superfluous to try, by the standard of theory, a part of the Constitution which is allowed on all hands to be the result, not of theory, but of a spirit of amity, and that mutual deference and concession which the peculiarity of our political situation rendered indispensable.

The selection of Senators by the State legislatures was another evidence of the quasi-sovereign nature of their role. They were not designed to represent people, or the people of a State, but the State itself. To quote Hamilton again:

> [The arrangement] is recommended by the double advantage of favoring a select appointment, and of giving to the state governments such an agency in the formation of the federal government as must secure the authority of the states, and may form a convenient link between the two systems.

The convention approved the appointment of Senators by the State legislatures in one of its earliest votes, on June 7, and by a margin of nine States to none. Madison and Wilson opposed the motion but both the Virginia and the Pennsylvania delegation votes were cast for it. Thus was the Senate transformed from what in Madison's mind was a representation of the people into a haven for State governments. Roger Sherman of Connecticut made this point clear when he defended equality of votes in the Senate "not so much as a security for the small states as for the state *governments,* which could not be preserved unless they were represented, and had a negative in the general government."

The intent of using equal votes in the Senate to give the States "a negative in the general government" was perhaps inadvertently undermined by a failure to require the two Senators from a State to cast a unified vote. Roll calls in the Senate call upon members, not upon States, and from the start it was quite possible for Senators from a State to vote against each other.

REPRESENTATION OF PRIVILEGED CLASSES IN SENATE

As I have already noted in Hamilton's explanation, the appointment of Senators by the State legislature was considered desirable for "favoring a select appointment." With Shays' rebellion fresh in their minds, many delegates were concerned that the new government should have some provision for protecting property and the rich. As Swanstrom observes: Many delegates "were divided merely on the question of the particular means by which the Senate could best be made to represent the wealthy, conservative interest." Agreement with this view cut across the usual divisions into which scholars classify the delegates. Small State delegates, large State delegates, southerners and northerners, nationalists and federalists, Randolph of large Virginia and Read of small Delaware, Hamilton and Madison among the nationalists and Dickinson and Ellsworth among the federalists, all agreed on this function of the Senate.

And for more than a century it did just that. According to Roy Swanstrom, "the Senate roll sounded almost like a 'Who's Who' of the wealthy and socially prominent of the day. Not only were the majority of these first 94 Senators men of handsome fortune, but this practice of sending wealthy individuals to the Senate extended to all parts of the country ... and to both parties."

During the latter part of the 19th century, the industrial revolution was marked by a new wave of Senatorial millionaires, led by the mine magnates of the far West. The World Almanac of 1902 listed 18 of the 90 Senators as millionaires. In 1906, one writer listed 25. The same year, George Haynes declared: "Never before in its history has the Senate been the target of such scathing criticism as during the past 15 years. On all sides is heard the charge that the Senate . . . is now the stronghold of the trusts and of corporate interests."

THE SENATE AS A CHECK ON EXECUTIVE POWER

Still a third function of the Senate was to be that of a council of wise men, chosen for longer terms than either the President or members of the House, older in years than House members, and with only a third standing for election at any one time. To bring these advantages to bear on the conduct of foreign policy, to the Senate was given the authority to advise and consent to the appointment of ambassadors and to ratify treaties.

The Federalist No. 62 referred to the qualifications of Senators thus:

> 1. The qualifications proposed for senators, as distinguished from those of representatives, consist in a more advanced age and a longer period of citizenship. A senator must be thirty years of age at least; as a representative must be twenty-five. And the former must have been a citizen for nine years; as seven years are required for the latter. The propriety of these distinctions is explained by the nature of the senatorial trust, which, requiring greater extent of information and stability of character, requires at the same time that the senator should have reached a period of life most likely to supply these advantages; and which, participating immediately in transactions with foreign nations, ought to be exercised by none who are not thoroughly weaned from the prepossessions and habits incident to foreign birth and education. . . .

In No. 63, we find that the Senate was designed to provide what the writer (either Hamilton or Madison) called "a due sense of national character," particularly with respect to international affairs.

> A fifth desideratum, illustrating the utility of a senate, is the want of a due sense of national character. Without a select and stable member of the government, the esteem of foreign powers will not only be forfeited by an unenlightened and variable policy, pro-

ceeding from the causes already mentioned, but the national councils will not possess that sensibility to the opinion of the world, which is perhaps not less necessary in order to merit, than it is to obtain, its respect and confidence.

An attention to the judgment of other nations is important to every government for two reasons: the one is, that, independently of the merits of any particular plan or measure, it is desirable, on various accounts, that it should appear to other nations as the offspring of a wise and honorable policy; the second is, that in doubtful cases, particularly where the national councils may be warped by some strong passion or momentary interest, the presumed or known opinion of the impartial world may be the best guide that can be followed. What has not America lost by her want of character with foreign nations; and how many errors and follies would she not have avoided, if the justice and propriety of her measures had, in every instance, been previously tried by the light in which they would probably appear to the unbiased part of mankind? . . .

A few paragraphs later, an expansion on this function of the Senate applies as well to our foreign policies as to our domestic policies:

As the cool and deliberate sense of the community ought, in all governments, and actually will in all free governments, ultimately prevail over the views of its rulers; so there are particular moments in public affairs when the people stimulated by some irregular passion, or some illicit advantage, or misled by the artful misrepresentations of interested men, may call for measures which they themselves will afterwards be the most ready to lament and condemn. In these critical moments, how salutary will be the interference of some temperate and respectable body of citizens, in order to check the misgiuded career, and to suspend the blow meditated by the people against themselves, until reason, justice, and truth can regain their authority over the public mind?

What bitter anguish would not the people of Athens have often escaped, if their government had contained so provident a safeguard against the tryanny of their own passions? Popular liberty might then have escaped the indelible reproach of decreeing to the same citizens the hemlock on one day and statues on the next.

So, as summed up by Constitutional historian Swanstrom, it was the intention of the delegates through the Senate "(1) to restrain the President, who might otherwise use the treaty power in a despotic and arbitrary manner . . .; (2) to give the President advice in the sense of information and counsel; (3) to defend the sovereignty of the States, of which the Senate was to be the special representative. . . ."

STATUS OF THESE FUNCTIONS TODAY

What can be said of these purposes today? I think it must be said that the 17th Amendment to the Constitution, more than any other except the 14th, altered the basic structure of the federal system.

In 1913, the issue was clearly posed: either the composition of the Senate must be changed, or it must be removed from the crucial processes of government. At that point, the Senate stood to become the equivalent of the House of Lords, or the French or Italian Senates: filled with men of age, wealth, and prestige, but without effective power.

The 17th Amendment took the other route. Instead of being shelved by the American people, the members of the United States Senate were made responsible to them. The amendment itself was preceded, I say with some pride, by the development in Oregon of a popular election of its Senators in 1901 and 1904, with a mere ratification by the state legislature of the choice made by the people. A decade later the change was accomplished for the entire nation.

Would the Founding Fathers have approved? Some, certainly, for no longer are Senators the ambassadors of their states. I am here not as Senator from Oregon, but as Senator from the people of Oregon. I represent not a state but the people of a state.

Madison and his friends, surely, would approve the 17th Amendment and the extent to which it has overcome the disabilities they so dreaded from the Great Compromise.

For as Senators came to represent people, they came to reflect the increasing homogeneity of the American people. Technology of transportation and communication, and the interrelation of our economy give a Senator from California a great plurality of constituents who came from somewhere else. State interests, as distinct from national interests, have never assumed the proportions that *regional* interests have assumed, and even regional differences are falling before a shifting population.

So, too, did the 17th Amendment largely destroy the function of the Senate as the bulwark of privileged classes. Today, wealth is helpful as a source of campaign funds, but not as a desirable quality in itself. The Senator who does not retain the confidence of his voting constituents does not remain in office, no matter how popular he may be with a malapportioned state legislature that has not yet faced the Supreme Court.

But at the same time, the 17th Amendment greatly strengthened the participation of the Senate in the legislative process. It strengthened the confidence of the people in it and removed once and for all the possibility that the United States would develop in the direction of a parliamentary system.

I would say that the Senate has not, however, fulfilled the role assigned to it in foreign policy. From its earliest days, it and the House have tended to delegate their international responsibilities to the President, including the war power. As early as Jefferson's Administration, Congress delegated to him authority to use whatever armed force might be necessary to put down the Barbary pirates. Similar resolutions aimed at Mexico in 1846, at Cuba in 1898, and at North Vietnam in 1964 failed to achieve their alleged objective of preventing war. In the case of Mexico, the resolution was used by the President to undertake acts that history regards as aggression and which plagued our relations with Mexico for a century after. Historical judgment is not yet in on the 1964 resolution but we do know it has served to expand and intensify the war in Asia. In the 1950s and 1960s, this practice of delegating the war power to the President has virtually eliminated the Senate as a check upon executive power in the conduct of foreign affairs.

The treaty power, likewise, has served to delegate to the executive sweeping authority that is exercised without further resort to Senate advice or action. The treaties whereby we incurred obligations of one kind or another to 42 countries are vague and unspecified in defining those obligations. But they are used, and misused, by the executive branch as it sees fit. In South Vietnam, what is now the fourth largest war in U.S. history is underway over a country with which we do not even have a direct treaty obligation, and which another treaty has been stretched to cover.

In the case of the Senate-ratified Rio treaty with the countries of Latin America, the American executive summarily shattered it in 1965 when, on the basis of hearsay evidence, he caused armies to march into the Dominican Republic!

These treaties, as ratified by the Senate, usually have contained mutual obligations, insofar as the obligations are defined. But here again, the mutuality of the obligations has been largely ignored by an executive seeking the free hand in foreign policy that the Constitution does not give it.

There has always been an elitist theory of foreign policy in this country, from Hamilton to the present. It holds that foreign affairs are best left to the experts and the technicians, that only those actually employed in the operating arms of our government's foreign policy structure have the knowledge or the competence to deal with these matters. This theory is advanced with increasing insistence in our own day.

I reject it, as the framers of the Constitution most certainly did. There is no question but that the President has large latitude in asserting initiatives. As John Jay pointed out in *The Federalist*, the unity of his office, its capacity for secrecy and dispatch, and its superior sources of information, not to mention the fact that it is always ready for action, give to the President great advantages. But these advantages cannot be pursued with a proper respect unless they are subjected to the practicalities of national representation. The nationalization of the Senate, I might add, ought to have increased its insistence upon fulfilling that function, for in the words of Congressman Abraham Lincoln, who opposed delegating the war power to Polk, "you give a President that power and you place our President where kings have always stood."

There is no need to present here a detailed history of the Senate's collaboration in its own decline as a check upon the President's conduct of foreign policy. Any modern history book and the daily newspaper relate the details of how it has allowed its advising and checking function to atrophy. Confronted by the admittedly immense complexities of modern world affairs, it added in recent years an aid agency and a disarmament agency to the State Department, and thousands of new employees to the executive branch to operate them, but it does nothing about expanding its own staff and facilities to confront the same problems. The Senate, in effect, has shrugged its collective shoulders and let whatever George is in the Presidency do it.

The Dominican intervention of 1965 was the most notorious example of what can result from those alleged advantages of action in foreign affairs which lie with the Presidency. It was also a notorious action of the kind the Senate was created to prevent, and it marked the extent to which the executive has learned to disregard the Senate in foreign policy.

The intervention was subjected to an inquiry by the Senate Foreign Relations Committee, and subsequently to a public critique by Committee Chairman, Senator Fulbright. The Senate's position in foreign affairs at that point of history was capsulized by the fact that Senator Fulbright's analysis was challenged as much on the ground of his right to say it as on the merits of what he said.

Hopefully, the Dominican post mortem marks the beginning of the Senate's long road back to constitutional responsibility. It was followed by public hearings on U.S. policy in Vietnam and then by a public review of American policy toward China that did more to enlighten the people about a crucial area of the world than any Senate action since the ratification of the NATO treaty.

More important, it bestirred a rigid bureaucracy that is a prisoner of its past in China and when left alone, seems unable to rid itself of the dogmas of history.

In the age when technology can make a small mistake a fatal one for the country and much of the world, the Senate must increase its participation in these decisions. It provides the forum for frank examination of what Senator Fulbright has called the old myths and new realities of the world. Above all, it must be "that temperate and respectable body of citizens" it was designed to be, "to check the misguided career, and to suspend the blow meditated by the people against themselves until reason, justice, and truth can regain their authority over the public mind."

If the Senate cannot maintain enough spirit to exert these intended powers in the field of foreign policy, then indeed that nightmare of the Framers of the Constitution—arbitrary, capricious, and tyrannous government—can well come to pass.

III. The Role of Executive Leadership

Senator Gale W. McGee

THE QUESTION OF EXECUTIVE POWER AND THE UNITED STATES Senate derives from a contradiction of historical experiences in the founding of the republic. For, while the American Revolution epitomized a sense or a craving of only a minor fraction of the population, its force was levied against the principle of executive power. The wrath of the rebels was pointed at the colonial governors and in its climax was directed at the head of King George III.

Once the Americans had won their independence, it was no surprise that they constructed a framework of government, the Articles of Confederation, that had no executive at all. The mistake, of course, in denying a head to the body politic was quickly illustrated the hard way in the tortuous years of the confederacy. The upshot of it was the attempt to correct this mistake by calling a new constitutional convention. The thing to be remembered in the Constitutional Convention, it seems to me, is that it was made up of an entirely different set of men and a different state of mind than that which prevailed at the signing of the Declaration of Independence. The men meeting in Philadelphia in 1787 were a far different group from those who met there in 1776. The Declaration was a liberal document; in general the Constitution was a conservative document. Neither group could have drafted the work of the other. In hindsight it is obvious to most of us there was then, and is now, a need for both groups.

But from the exuberance of the liberals in the great Declaration, the conservatives in Philadelphia in 1787 had shifted to the hard fact of the need for executive power. So out of it came a Constitution, the full meaning of which would remain the subject of considerable controversy for the remaining days of the republic down to our own present moment. And since 1787, our history has been dotted, without any set pattern, by the regimes of strong presidents, of average presidents, and of weak presidents. American historians do not always agree on the great issues of the time any more than on their assessments of the past; but a poll among them a few years back did reveal a near consensus on the designation of the "great" Presidents. Some five or six American Presidents were so marked, including George Washington, Thomas Jefferson, Andrew Jackson, Abraham Lincoln, Woodrow Wilson, and Franklin Roosevelt. To mention them in particular is to point up a conspicuous circumstance; namely, that they happened more as phenomena of accident rather than consequences of institutional design. The fact that each of these men, as strong executives, came at a moment of crisis is not to suggest either that the presidency was capable, automatically, of producing strong presidents in time of need.

Indeed, there were other critical eras of American history when the Constitution or the institutions of the republic failed to produce the necessary strong executives. This was notably true at the time of the war of 1812; during the decade leading to the Civil War; amid the crises of the war with Spain in 1898; as well as the desperate days of the 1920's, when strong presidents might have made a significant difference. But whether the presidents were strong or weak, or regardless of what the times may have cried out for, one theme constantly emerged—the constant rivalry and controversy between the executive and the legislature, or Congress. Neither seemed to trust the other. Each regarded the other with considerable jealousy.

By our own decade of the 1960's, it has become abundantly clear to most of us, in my judgment, that executive leadership no longer can be left to chance: That we can no longer gamble on the "accident," the good luck, to produce a strong man in the White House in a time of great need. Particularly since the advent of World War II, it has become more and more obvious that we have to take the steps necessary to insure that a democracy such as ours can always command the kind of leadership that the times require. While that leadership must always remain the subject of legislative scrutiny and judgment (I do not propose that we downgrade the old principles of checks and balances), it is equally imperative that the concept of those principles be updated in accord with the rapidly shifting age of which we are now a part.

The emergence of the need for a stronger executive in our system of government has intensified the traditional rivalry that has historically strained the relations from time to time between the two ends of Pennsylvania Avenue. In part those strains are historical: They were put there to be strains; namely, to reflect a lurking distrust of a strong executive. But in part these strains have been intensified by a sense of jealousy. The longer some men remain in the Senate of the United States, the greater the tendency on the part of some of them to seek to justify the importance of their long tenure or to assert greater and greater authority, regardless of the consequences. In the general processes of government itself an element of jealousy among the rival branches of the government cannot properly accentuate the right needs for better government; and yet that jealousy is there, largely because the public still elects mortals to the United States Senate. Human nature being what it is, there is no formula that I know of to eliminate this subjective element of political jealousy.

The rise of the power of the Federal Government in authority, in contrast to state and local authority, is that factor which, more than any other, sharply intensified the traditional rivalries between the executive and the Senate. The need for greater Federal authority because of the mobility of people, because of the growth of economic power which transcends state lines, because of the overlapping of social responsibilities, and because of the ease with which people get around and get about, all combine to leave Federal power as the only reasonable alternative in dealing with many of the great questions of our day.

State governments, in our time, have been found inadequate to cope with many of the questions because so few problems any more can be confined within the borders of a single state, nor in many instances even within the confines of a local region. And to neglect them or to return them back to the states, would, in fact, be forfeiting the responsibility for doing something about them at all.

Constitutional safeguards on executive power written into the

Constitution, do create the opportunities for an individual Senator to assert an authority and a power greatly beyond his numbers, his number being one. And the power of a single Senator to restrain the executive, to acquire a bargaining position with the executive or to hamstring the executive, is still very considerable. And I would raise the question as to whether we can afford a completely free-reining operation in this regard. So I advance the contention, as a member of the Senate, that the need for increasing executive power is very much the requirement of the day. It is heresy, I suppose, for a member of the most elite club in the world (some say) to make a statement of that nature; but we are here not to promulgate a comfortable private preserve but, I assume, for the purpose of trying to strengthen the fabric of the republic of which we are a part and the political system in which we believe.

We should be gathered here in these deliberations, in other words, as sort of scientists of the architecture of government, as constructive critics of that framework in the hopes that our give-and-take may help us to make it better, not to preserve certain of its functions for the pleasure of given individuals but to make it mean even more in the latter part of the Twentieth Century. I submit that the increase in the responsibilities of the executive, in the power of the executive, stems not alone from the growth of the Federal Government (although that in itself is considerable): There is no other single repository of responsibility that could be held accountable for what happens, given the complexities of the needs of a country as vast and as sprawling as the United States of America. No Senator really has that common responsibility to so many at all levels of the economy, in all segments of the social framework, and across the full spectrum of philosophy as well. I will have something to say at a later point about the new Senator that I think should emerge in these times. But suffice to say that only the President is elected by all of the people and thus, by the very nature of the problems that are ours, is the one person to whom we can assign responsibility for getting something done for all of the people.

The need to pin down responsibility in these rapidly changing times is, then, a second reason for increasing the power of the President. One of the most fool-proof hideouts for political criminals in the world is in our political legislative bodies. There the chances to pass the buck to somebody else, to duck the responsibility for failure and, conversely, to seize the credit for success, is one of the dilemmas that face us. At the same time, this capability of disguising responsibility or evading it, is the kind of old political game that was played for so long in the Nineteenth Century, but one which we can ill-afford in this portion of the Twentieth Century. You can duck responsibility within your committee (and we have all done it); you can blame somebody else's committee; you can disappear behind the facade of your party allegiance, or of the philosophical group within your party to which you belong; or you can blame it on the other House; and if none of those happens to fit or work, you can dump it onto the shoulders of bureaucracy and red tape downtown. Because of these and other ready opportunities for evading public responsibility, it is all the more imperative that there be some one place where responsibility can be measured and judged fairly if our system of representative government is to keep up with the pace of the changing times. And I respectfully submit that the only possible check on that kind of responsibility can be measured at the executive level.

The third reason for the need to increase executive power at the other end of Pennsylvania Avenue, in addition to the growth of the Federal Government, and in addition to the requirements of pinning responsibilities in very complex times, is surely the new role of the United States in international politics, particularly since World War II. After that war, for the first time in our history, we found ourselves strangely on the front line of the world. Until then we always had an ocean that was a comforting barrier between us and international trouble. Until then we had others on the front line who were generally friendly and whom we could count to fight a delaying action, until we could make up our minds. Likewise, it was formerly the case in our history whenever there was a war, usually in Europe which was the center of power politics in the "good old days," that we could casually view the two sides involved and then choose the one that seemed to be closest to our national interest. But once more, after World War II, for the first time in our history, we emerged as one of the two sides. No longer can we enjoy the luxury of choice. The rose was pinned on us. And these harsh facts, emerging from the ruins and in the victory of World War II, command a new look at this question of executive power and the U. S. Senate.

Emerging with that in the wake of the War, likewise was the obvious necessity of acquiring an executive power that could deal decisively with any one of several monolithic states. The President cannot say to a foreign potentate, for example, "Well, I can't discuss this with the Prime Minister or the Premier (who may be figureheads in a dictatorship) until I can go back and sound out public opinion. Moreover, I will have to thrash it out in the Congress before I can take a stand." Obviously, that would place a representative government such as ours at a considerable disadvantage, where the need in these times on the international stage often requires forthright and quick decisions. And so the advent of our emergence into a world of strong governments or strong government leaders, dictators, if you will, requires that we try to strengthen the freedom of action on the part of the President, not for the purpose of making him a dictator but to preserve for him the latitude of decision-making. The advent of national elections would still be a sufficient repository for popular checks and balances on the wisdom of his actions.

The proliferation of nations constitutes a fourth need for increasing executive power as well. We now have more new nations in the world since World War II than we had a total of nations in all the history of the world up to that time. This proliferation requires a sense of decision-making or contact and higher level of communication that can ill-afford the delays, the procrastinations, and the lack of legislators informed on many different areas of the world so characteristic of legislative processes of the first half even of our present Century.

And finally, the emergence of a nuclear world, a world that commands a capability for obliterating itself for the first time in the history of Man, makes the obvious point that stronger and stronger executive responsibility is the one more likely direction in which to move if we are to hold a tight rein on nuclear threats.

Now, having mentioned these general principles that I believe argue for increased executive power, let me mention a case or two in which, in my judgment, the Legislature—the Senate which has a special role in foreign policy of the United States according to the Constitution—has not exactly risen to great heights of statesmanship. About two years ago we had an issue that was posed that involved extending the Food for Peace Program to Mr. Nasser in Cairo. At about that same time, Mr. Nasser had made some very nasty comments about the United States and, as a result, the outbursts on the floor of the Senate of the United States were most vituperative and scarcely statesmanlike. But the real issue in this, it seems to me, was whether a commitment that had been made much earlier should be canceled and whether it was wise ever to project American policy out of a sense of pique. A leader of anyone's world can hardly afford to develop foreign policy based on anger toward the head of another government—a Nasser or a Sukarno. A policy, to be enduring, must be developed because it is right and even wise. After all, the people of Egypt or of Indonesia will still be around long after their leaders are gone. Emotions or hates or passing whims are lame excuses for a foreign policy.

And yet, because the Senate of the United States does represent a constituency, it is understandable that many Senators do not really believe what sometimes they feel compelled to say on the floor of the Senate. Nevertheless, the temptation to make political hay by saying rather flagrant things about the head of government in Cairo represents a low-level political luxury which our Nation can ill-afford in these times.

But the most frustrating of all, I suppose, is the matter of foreign aid. Once more, as it has often been said, because foreign aid has no local constituency here at home, it acquires fewer and fewer friends in Washington. And the Congress asserts, year after year, its "right" to go through the political orgy of examining each critical detail of the foreign aid program. Congress hamstrings the program as a result, not only in the manpower time that is expended but in the simple fact that it is impossible to project a long-range plan of action. And here is one of the areas where I think a very fine case can be made, and has been made, for a program that can extend for three or four or five years without the threat of serious interruption.

A program that can only proceed by fits and starts depending upon the whims of the Congress in any one year can hardly acquire a solid foundation or create a yardstick of measurement for its effectiveness. In fact, it has built-in limitations as a result, almost automatically, that would prejudice the chances for its success. And so here again the Senate, by reverting to its constitutional right to review everything the Executive does every year, has refused—until now—to permit the kind of approach to the problem of foreign aid that, I think, the times demand. But those are specific illustrations that I offer for the purposes of making the point that the nature of these times that are so filled with crisis commands a new look at the distribution of powers—particularly in the realm of Foreign Relations.

What can we do about it now? Well, we are doing some things: First, take a look at the Executive himself. I think it has been of some help that the last two Presidents have come from the Senate. This is not to suggest that we can find future Presidents only in the Senate. Rather, it reflects the changing times. Historically, until 1960, it was virtually impossible to elect a United States Senator to the Presidency of the United States. Many outstanding Senators had tried. The more common political pathway to the White House started in the governor's mansion. But the changing times have brought a new emphasis on the Senate so that in 1960 and again in 1964, the candidates of both parties had had a long experience in the United States Senate. I think this reflects the rightful concern of the country, more and more, on international questions. But it has had a salutary effect in regard to executive power and the Senate in that recently we have had men in the White House who understood the "greatest deliberative body" and, in some instances, were actually a part of the Club. The result has been closer liaison between the two ends of Pennsylvania Avenue. That does not make it a part—a permanent part—of our formula for the future; but it has helped, it seems to me, in the necessary transitional phase from, say, 1960 down through the years immediately ahead of us into new concepts about executive responsibility and the use of executive power.

Both President Kennedy and President Johnson have very generously resorted to the device, in addition, of briefing Members of Congress on the great questions. Until this began, the briefings were ordinarily confined to the appropriate committee—the Foreign Relations Committee, or the Armed Services Committee, or the Appropriations Committee, and no more. But the men who came into the White House directly from the Senate had a sense of understanding the need for getting fifty-one votes or sixty-seven votes in order to get a measure passed rather than just a vote from a single committee. And thus, beginning with Mr. Kennedy and carried even further by Mr. Johnson, there has been a conscious effort to brief very carefully all interested members of both the Senate and the House, but particularly the Senate. I say all willing segments because it isn't mandatory that a Senator attend the briefings, but most of them show up.

Likewise, from the Executive end of the street, Secretary of State Dean Rusk, in my judgment, has done the most notable job of any Secretary we know of in history of maintaining a close rapport with the members of the Senate. Rusk was never a Senator. As a matter of fact, he had that vastly mystifying limitation of having been a professor; but he has been an extremely astute politician even so, and the great care that he has taken to fill in Members of Congress with background on the decisions that he thinks had to be made has had an exceedingly useful effect "on the Hill." His predecessor some years earlier, John Foster Dulles, did not go that far. Mr. Dulles was a very capable Secretary of State, but he carried his foreign policy in his hat. And even though he served—albeit briefly—in the Senate of the United States on an appointive basis, he never fully exercised the opportunities for briefing the members of the Senate on what he was going to do before he did it. Instead, he was continually explaining "why" after the fact. The psychology of this approach is of considerable importance.

Finally,—not only because of the Senatorial backgrounds of the two recent Presidents—because of the special efforts that have been made to stage background briefings for the members of the Senate, both by the President and by the Secretary of State or the Secretary of Defense, in particular, there has been established a far superior liaison system between the Executive Branch and the Legislative Branch of the Government.

Some six or seven years ago the administration was trying to get through a treaty on the Antarctic. The Antarctic Treaty proposed, among other things, that the Russians and the Americans try some joint scientific experiments in the Antarctic. It was hoped that this might pioneer other enterprises of this sort on a more meaningful scale. The Treaty was assumed to be so good in purpose and so harmless in content that there could be no opposition. But the moment the word "Russian" appeared somewhere in the discussions, two-thirds of the Senators were on their feet trying to speak against it. No one had taken the precaution of preparatory briefing work with the members of the Senate to explain it. This incident did much to provoke recognition of the need for much closer liaison between the legislators and the President. As a result, the outcome has been a far more successful legislative endeavor by the Executive, due in substantial measure to the skillful tactical leadership of Larry O'Brien, whose responsibility this was under both Kennedy and Johnson.

Now, having said that about the Executive, what can we do with the Senate of the United States? What should its role be? I submit that the role of the Senate in the future shall become more and more advisory. Until now, the Senate has initiated a few notable constructive programs in foreign policy; but they have been less and less numerous as the times have become more and more complicated. I think this trend will continue and ought to continue, with the Senate becoming an advisory body rather than an initiating body.

It is important, moreover, that we continue the present trend of selecting Senators on the state level more and more for their national or international positions than for their local or state views. A personal illustration will make the general point.

In the Wyoming U.S. Senate race of 1958, I was running for my first political office, with no previous political experience in government, having been for twenty-three years a professor of American history and international relations. My opponent, the incumbent, had held public office at all levels for more than a quarter century. Among other things, he was a clear-cut, undisguised isolationist in foreign policy. The central issue of the contest was his indictment that: "Gale McGee knows more about the world than he knows about Wyoming." Instead of avoiding the charge, I met it head-on. Note the date—1958. The Russians had launched Sputnik, and heretofore isolated Westerners were suddenly discovering that there was in all truth no place to hide. The results of that election reflected at least in part the updating in the public mind of what a U.S. Senator had to stand for.

Put it another way: I am from a very small state. In population, 350,000—scarcely the equivalent of a Washington precinct in numbers. Yet the state of Wyoming has two United States Senators—the same as New York, or Texas, or California, with a special responsibility in foreign policy which I think ought to continue as a formula. Even though I am from Wyoming, I receive more mail from the other forty-nine states than I get from my home state. This suggests the steady emergence of the public's image of the new United States Senator from any state; namely, that he is first of all a Senator of the United States and, second, a Senator from an individual state.

Related to this changing image of the new Senator is the Senator's counterpart—those who still hedge on the shape of the future by pretending to withhold their own judgments in foreign affairs until "weighing" the mail from home. This is not only irresponsible, it is downright cowardly. On all national and international questions, it seems to me, it is sheer political weakness for any United States Senator to cloak his uncertainty or indecision behind the excuse that he has to see what his constituents want him to do. A man elected to the United States Senate more and more has to take a stand and then lead in shaping opinion rather than follow from the local constituency point of view. The local constituents should make a great difference, at all times, on questions that are peculiar to their area. But the average constituent cannot possibly know the background of the Vietnam conflict or what happens when the highways into West Berlin are closed, or be informed on most of the great crisis questions of our times. On the other hand, a Senator ought to find out and provide leadership. He ought to know more in depth on the big questions than do his people at home—or be fired from his job. This is one of the approaches that has to be re-emphasized in the days ahead. Too often the Senate has been a millstone around the neck of the policy-makers in times of crisis. More and more, this kind of Senatorial obstruction or handicap must be reduced.

Finally, I suggest in regard to the Senate that while we are concerned about modernizing the Senate, I really think it is more important that we modernize the Senators. We tend to blame too many things that go wrong in the Senate on the machinery. And this is a pleasant way to avoid responsibility. The machinery of legislation cannot talk back. The real answer to most of the problems of the Senate is to be found among the Senators themselves. I think, for example, that they should be required to indulge less and less in housekeeping chores which take most of their time now and more and more in a little statesmanship. This can be done through expanded staff. This can be done through other service arrangements that will take care of this chore work—perhaps in the Executive departments, if necessary. Senators spend too much time now with minutia, big for the person who made the request, perhaps, but small in terms of the pressures imposed on the Senator by the world in which we live.

Equally important, the new Senator of the 1960's should be encouraged, even forced, into grasping more and more of the "big picture" of our time; and he cannot do it in a typical day at the office, racing from committee to committee or from vote to vote without time to read and reflect. I am often asked what I miss most from my more than twenty years of academic life, I think it is the opportunity to read and reflect. When you have to do most of your reading by trying to catch headlines on the way to work; or when Herblock becomes your substitute for speedreading, I believe it illustrates how tight are the pressures and how severe are the impositions on one's time. At this special moment in human history, the world seems literally convulsed by overlapping revolutions, the consequences and directions of which remain mysterious. Also at this same moment, the Senate of the United States finds itself cast in the role of influencing, and even shaping, those forces. Yet that greatest deliberative body in the world is so weighed down with kitchen chores that its members have precious little time to think big. Nearly every freshman Senator arrives on the scene with a personal reservoir of knowledge and experience to draw upon to support his first legislative efforts. But after a very few sessions of Congress at most that reservoir is emptied. No opportunity now exists for the Senator to replenish the drained reserves. This is taking place at a sort of crossroads of history, when the profile of the future of the human race may be even now being sketched. Our Senator, however, is so busy "shooting from the hip" on day-to-day questions that he has lost sight of the whys and wherefores of nuclear age and world problems. His sense of perspective invariably becomes distorted or just plain disappears. This process must be reversed—and soon.

Recently, I proposed to the Congress that we create Senatorial sabbaticals, similar to those in the academic profession, for the obvious purpose of giving a Senator a chance to read and reflect and to recharge his batteries. At a given interval to be determined by wise men, every Senator would be required to leave Washington for six months to one year. During that time he would not be allowed to visit the Nation's Capitol or to return to his home state. In short, he would be required to stay out of reach of both lobbyists and constituents. His sojourn should take him to a mountain top, an island, or best of all to one of the great campuses of some of the fine institutions of higher learning around the world, to refresh and refurbish his mental proclivities and enrich his philosophy in order to acquire, hopefully, a better grasp of such queries as: "Whither mankind?" Not a care should he have about the substance of a bill to be drafted or a vote to be cast. Rather, his total obsession might well become that of critically examining the kind of world in which he hoped to survive. It is imperative that United States Senators, more and more, be crowded into keeping in focus the whole canvas of the future; be pressed into fitting into the perspective of our times the role in which we find ourselves at the present moment. This, in my judgment, would help update Senators.

But, in the final analysis, it comes down to the voter himself. To be sure, the voter is becoming increasingly sophisticated as some recent elections have shown. He still has a considerable distance to go, however. He has not only to come to expect the right kind of performance from a Senator, but to *demand* it. And so while it might even be convenient to blame some Senators for things that go wrong, very often those Senators are simply trying to reflect the moods of the voters. And so in the last analysis the voter himself has to come of age, has to catch up with the last half of the Twentieth Century if we are to stay on top of the present and even anticipate some of the future.

These, then, represent some of the elements supporting my belief in the need for greater executive power at a time of frightening, if exciting, international responsibilites.

# IV. The Role of the Senate in Determining Foreign Policy

Senator John J. Sparkman

IT MAY BE A LITTLE DIFFICULT TO DRAW A VERY CLEAR AND easily distinguished line as to just where the authority of the Senate of the United States begins and where it leaves off in the field of foreign policy. But there are some things that we may keep in mind—that is, that in the Constitution itself, the Senate is designated as the body to advise and consent to the appointment of representatives of the President in foreign countries, and also to ratify treaties. That is basically the authority for the Senate's role in the field of foreign affairs.

In modern times, the advice of the Senate has never been sought with respect to ambassadorial appointments, though on occasion the President and Secretary of State may seek the recommendations of individual Senators in specific instances. Sometimes, as well, individual Senators may volunteer recommendations. That is done quite frequently, in fact. Ambassadorial nominations are almost never rejected by the Senate, and very few are even debated, despite occasional misgivings which Senators may hold privately. The Senate normally presumes in favor of a nominee and, further, believes that the President is entitled to have the individual of his choice serving in an ambassadorial post, unless there are very compelling reasons to the contrary.

I think we can see the reason for that. Under the Constitution, the President of the United States is the one man in our governmental system charged with the responsibility of carrying on relations with foreign countries. And the ambassador to each foreign country is the President's personal representative to that country. It is very similar to the situation with reference to the approval of the President's nominations for Cabinet members. Nominations for Cabinet Members have been turned down at times, but very rarely, because the Cabinet is the intimate family, governmentally speaking, to help the President in running the affairs of the country. And it is generally felt that he is entitled to have the persons he wants in that small, close group.

During the time I have been on the Foreign Relations Committee the President has withdrawn a few nominations for ambassadorial posts after learning that Senators had serious misgivings about the nominees. I do not recall, however, that we have ever turned down an Ambassador on a record vote. As a matter of fact, ordinarily there is no roll call vote in the Senate on such appointments, but only a voice vote.

The advice and consent function is much more important with respect to treaties. The Senate has sometimes formally advised the President to negotiate a particular treaty—as it did with the Vandenberg Resolution which laid the groundwork for the North Atlantic Treaty. Initiatives of the sort by the Senate are rare, but do occur.

More frequently, however, the Senate's advice is given through one or more informal consultations between officials of the State Department and members of the Foreign Relations Committee. A classic example of this was the series of meetings that John Foster Dulles held with the Far Eastern Subcommittee of the Senate Foreign Relations Committee. I was Chairman of that Subcommittee. Mr. Dulles was negotiating the Japanese Peace Treaty.

Probably no other treaty in history required more time, more work, and more maneuvering to get promulgated, largely because of the large number of nations involved. Mr. Dulles went from capital to capital—to London, to Paris, to Moscow, to the capitals of all the leading nations—to get their ideas. Then he tried to pull those ideas together and revisited the capitals to see if he could work out an agreement. Every time he returned home he would call me and say, "I'd like to sit down with your Subcommittee." We had lots of breakfasts together. Often we had lunch or dinner together. We met morning, noon, and night. I have often said that this was one of the finest examples of two things, first, cooperation between the Executive and the Legislative, and second, bipartisanship. Mr. Dulles was a Republican working for a Democratic

President. Our Committee was Democratic, yet the Republicans on the Subcommittee went right along with it. We always had good attendance, and many ideas for the Treaty were born in these Subcommittee meetings.

The Japanese Peace Treaty was, of course, one of the most complex and significant of modern times. Yet even in more routine matters, the State Department in recent years has almost always at least notified the Senate Foreign Relations Committee in advance of a treaty negotiation.

Unlike the situation with regard to the nomination of Ambassadors, the Senate's ratification of a treaty is not given lightly. Sometimes it is not given at all, and oftentimes, when it is given, reservations are adopted as a part of the treaty.

The Senate rarely rejects a treaty. In fact, ordinarily, if the treaty is not acceptable to the Foreign Relations Committee, it simply does not act on the treaty. Some treaties have been left hanging before our Committee for several years. Some are there now. The Genocide convention, for instance, has been hanging since 1949. A number of the treaties that have not been acted upon are not particularly objectionable, but perhaps things were not right for them at the time they were presented. The Committee may even favor a treaty, but fail to bring it before the Senate simply because it fears that the required two-thirds affirmative vote cannot be mustered. In such circumstances, a positive rejection by the Senate might do more harm to United States foreign relations than inaction, and the Committee prefers to take the blame itself for its failure to push for ratification.

Treaties of trade and commerce formerly could get snagged that way, but that has not been true in recent years because treaties of friendship, trade, and commerce with nations have been virtually standardized. We know quite well what is going to be in a treaty of that kind when it comes before us. We examine it carefully to make certain that it observes the guidelines that have been laid down by the Senate, and oftentimes, by the Foreign Relations Committee. This indicates the power that the Senate, and particularly the Senate Foreign Relations Committee, may have upon a treaty.

In addition to the Constitutional function of advice and consent, the Senate shares with the House several powers which impinge directly or indirectly on the determination of foreign policy.

When I came to the House of Representatives nearly thirty years ago its Foreign Affairs Committee had little importance. In fact, sometimes it was difficult to get members to go on that committee. But all that was changed. It started changing before World War II, when we got into the enactment of new neutrality laws. It started to build up as most important legislation came up, such as Lend Lease. Lend Lease was not something that could be handled by the Senate alone. The House sat in on it—not on the ratification of any treaty, but on implementing it—because it called for appropriations, and the House contended strongly that while it does not control, it is an equal partner, at least, when it comes to appropriations. So the House Foreign Affairs Committee today, except for the matter of confirming the appointment of Ambassadors and ratifying treaties, is pretty much a co-equal member in the handling of foreign policy, because so much of it is handled on the basis of legislation that is required to put it into effect.

The powers we share include, first, the power to declare war. This is steadily diminishing in practical importance. Many people, I think, believe that probably there never will be another declared war; unless a declaration serves to confirm what has already been done. The place of the declaration of war has in some measure been taken by the resolution authorizing the President to take such action as he might see fit in a threatening situation—such as was passed at President Eisenhower's request when war was threatened in the Formosa Straits in 1955. But, as I have argued on the floor of the Senate myself, the President has the needed power without such a resolution, and has used it in a number of instances dating back at least to President Truman's actions in the Greek-Turkish program and the inception of the Korean War.

Second is the power of the purse. As foreign policy involves more and more activities that cost money, this is steadily increasing in importance.

Then, there is the power to authorize foreign affairs programs, which the President could not carry out in the absence of legislation. For instance, I mentioned Lend Lease. Since the war, foreign aid, overseas information activities, and many others could be named. This power necessarily carries with it the power to place conditions and restrictions on the way such programs are carried out.

Fourth, the balance of the broad range of Congress' legislative powers, even legislation of a purely domestic character, may affect the position of the United States in the world, or the ability of the President to carry out foreign policies. Tax legislation may affect foreign investment or the ability of United States industries to compete around the world. Legislation in the field of labor-management relations may have the same effect through its impact on the cost of production of United States industries. Domestic agricultural programs directly affect foreign affairs through determining, among other things, whether the United States will produce surplus agricultural commodities to be used in connection with foreign aid programs—and so on.

In a system of checks and balances, Constitutional relationships between the different branches inherently are essentially negative. One branch can prevent another from doing something, but cannot force it to do something. The Senate can advise the President to make a treaty, but he cannot force the Senate to consent to one. The Congress can frustrate a program of the President by refusing to appropriate the necessary funds, but it cannot force the President to initiate a program against his will by appropriating funds which he has not requested. A clear example of this occurred under President Truman. Foreign aid money was voted to Spain by the Congress, and the President impounded it. In this case the President used his power through negative action.

If repeated constitutional impasses are to be avoided, this essentially negative set of relationships must operate on the basis of a broad consensus. To a considerable degree, this consensus is achieved through a variety of informal contacts which may range from White House conferences between the President and Senate leaders to casual telephone conversations between individual Senators and officials of the State Department.

The Foreign Relations Committee is the Senate's chosen instrument in this field as well as in more formal mechanisms for consideration of foreign policy questions. (So all-pervasive is the influence of Senate actions on foreign policy, however, that the Foreign Relations Committee is by no means the exclusive instrument. Trade legislation goes to Finance; disposal of surplus agricultural commodities to Agriculture, and so on.)

The Foreign Relations Committee takes its role as the Senate's foreign policy agent seriously, including its function of legislative oversight under the Legislative Reorganization Act. The Committee operates through subcommittees based on geography. I am now Chairman of the European Subcommittee, which holds consultations quite often with members of the Executive branch. Often the President will call us over, or we will go to the State Department, or Secretary Rusk will come up to the Hill or will send some other officials. They usually keep us very well briefed on what is going on. The Committee, however, must necessarily limit itself to consideration of broad policy questions. It is incapable of overseeing the myriad details of day-to-day foreign policy operations.

This is so and should be for many reasons. For administration to be effective, responsibility must be centralized through a single chain of command leading to the President.

In addition, members of the Foreign Relations Committee are far too busy to deal with anything except broad policy questions. Every Senator is a member of at least two, and in many cases more, committees. The Senators who serve on Foreign Relations also serve on Finance, Banking and Currency, Agriculture, and the like, and have many duties to occupy their time in those committees. Further, every Senator has to have at least some knowledge of legislation that is considered by the Senate but reported by committees of which he is not a member. Finally, and most important in a very practical way, every Senator has to attend to the problems of his State. This means that Senators are spread very thin. They simply cannot devote very much attention to any single program without neglecting another of equal importance.

It is frequently argued that Senators could alleviate this problem by providing themselves with larger and more expert staffs. But this would create an even more severe problem of a different kind—a problem of supervising and managing the staff. A larger staff could, of course, produce more voluminous research memoranda for Senators—but Senators don't have time to read all the research memoranda they get now. The problem is not to find a way for Senators to get more facts; the problem is for Senators to know what to do with the facts they have.

This is a problem of judgment, not expertise. Few Senators and few Senate staff members are experts in the academic sense—Paul Douglas, a distinguished former professor of economics, was a conspicuous exception. Many Senators have a detailed understanding of one or two fields of legislation; but—again with a few exceptions—a Senator usually becomes an "expert" at the expense of neglecting something else. After all, you don't have to know everything about fur seals to pass on a fisheries treaty with Japan.

As I said, if this system of ours is to work, it must be based on broad consensus. This is true not only as between the legislative and executive branches of government, but also as between the government and the people. Its part in helping to achieve such a consensus is one of the most important, and at the same time one of the most elusive, roles which the Senate plays in determining foreign policy.

I once spoke to the National War College on "What Influence Does the Public Have?" Rather strange to say, the public does have considerable influence on foreign policy in this country. I suppose it probably has greater effect than in any other nation. Of course, this is limited by the fact that the public does not and cannot know a good part of what is said and done in foreign affairs. The public simply cannot be made privy to a great deal of information regarding these things. I regret that that is true, but think that it is absolutely necessary if we are to get the results that we desire. The game of diplomacy requires great art and great skill. You simply do not call your signals out loud.

Despite this handicap, the Senate is in several ways one of this country's great forums for the exploration and illumination of public issues. This function is frequently served by debate in the Senate itself. It is also served through committee hearings, studies, and reports. Over the past few years, for example, the Senate Foreign Relations Committee has explored the questions involved in the East-West trade issue in several hearings. The Committee has received the views, and asked questions of, members of the Cabinet as well as scholars, bankers, and businessmen. The Committee's role here has not been crucial, but it has made a contribution to the growing public discussion.

In the long run, no foreign policy is any better than the public understanding and support upon which it rests. The Senate serves as a two-way bridge between government and people. It both leads and follows. It tests, in debate, the policies of the President. It helps to interpret, to the President, the thoughts and ideas of the people and to give these form and substance. On occasion, it even generates original proposals of its own which set off equally lively discussions in the planning councils of the Department of State and in the editorial pages and college campuses of the country.

When, out of all this mixed-up interplay, a policy emerges, no one can say who thought of it first. But more often than not, the Senate has played an important role.

The final measure of consensus in a system such as ours, which is organized on the basis of two great political parties, is bipartisanship or, as the late Senator Arthur Vandenberg used to call it, unpartisanship. Senator Vandenberg, although at first an isolationist, became a great convert to bipartisanship, and the results of his effort have been marked time and again in the votes and actions of the Senate.

I would like to pay tribute to Senator Vandenberg by closing with some of the words of his last public speech on September 15, 1949. In it he proudly summed up the results of his bipartisanship:

> It seems to me that our basic pattern is clear. The Senate of the United States ratified the United Nations Charter by a vote of 89 to 2. It ratified the Interamerican Rio Treaty by a vote of 72 to 1. It approved the initial Marshall Plan by a vote of 83 to 17. It adopted Senate Resolution 239 [the Vandenberg Resolution] fifteen months ago, demanding more effective strength for all of these, by a vote of 64 to 4. It ratified the North Atlantic Pact by a vote of 82 to 13. . . .
>
> There is a powerful consistency in these attitudes. They asserted, and I believe they still assert our general and very deep convictions that the Free World must work together for its common interest in collective peace and that no other character of peace can be dependable in this foreshortened world.

The spirit of bipartisanship so powerfully cultivated during Senator Vandenberg's Chairmanship of the Senate Foreign Relations Committee has continued under the able and distinguished chairmen who have followed him. Even today, while the Senate discusses the various sides of our position in Vietnam, the debate is not partisan. It is a further extension of the Senate's historic role in foreign policy—as advisor, as interpreter of national opinion, and as great forum for the airing of public issues.

The Senator as Politician

On his way back to the Capitol after delivering his lecture, one Senator remarked to the student who was driving him, "I love politics; I think about it all the time. There is nothing else like it. You never get tired of it."

Perhaps not all senators would subscribe to these sentiments, but all must be adept at the political game. In the essays in this section, two senators describe how a Senator attains and keeps his seat, and how he maintains communication with and support from his constituency. Both display the variety of policy issues and group interests to which a Senator must be ready to respond. Beyond this, however, both demonstrate the demand which the voters make for a sense of personal attention, warmth, and concern on the part of elected representatives toward their constituents. The handshake of a Morton or the individualized letter of a Scott are parts of a process of making a remote and complex governmental machine appear close and human to its citizens.

But we demand a little more of our senators than that they be human. As Senator Morton asserts, they must also project stature. Their appearance and their actions should suggest simultaneously a sympathy toward the common man and an ability surpassing his own. Is the image of stature the source of the freedom to employ independent judgment which both senators claim, or might it be, in part at least, a consequence of its exercise?

V. Senatorial Campaigning

Senator Thruston B. Morton

THE FIRST THING TO UNDERSTAND IN DISCUSSING SENATORIAL campaigns is simply that the candidates are individual with all the differences that implies and, also, the constituencies involved differ. Consequently, there is no single formula for success in all campaigns. Once I was asked on behalf of a colleague seeking election whether he could find a book detailing the elements of a winning race. There are plenty of books, but none can ever set forth the winning combination for more than one given election. Differences in men, time, and place militate against it.

Nevertheless, I have discovered, in practicing politics for many years, that there are certain common denominators among all, or nearly all, victorious candidates for the Senate. These are: stature, intimate awareness of the problems of their states, a good sense of public relations and, in most cases, previous political experience.

The first quality is the ability to project stature. I do not mean physical stature necessarily, but the sense that the candidate is above the normal run of politicians—that he has an intellectual capacity and a knowledge of public affairs that go beyond the borders of his state to encompass national affairs and international affairs. He must appear to deserve to win.

At the same time, he must be intimately aware of the problems of his state—and they may be varied. This is sometimes difficult. I had a narrow squeak taking my first election to the Senate. Previously, I had served in the House for three terms and then a stint as Assistant Secretary of State under the Eisenhower Administration. As a Member of the House I had represented a district which was strictly metropolitan. I had, for example, no problems with agriculture—my greatest agriculture problem as a Congressman was finding some flower seeds for the window boxes! I had no contact with coal mining, a great enterprise to the East and West of my district. I was unfamiliar with public works projects and proposals in the greater part of Kentucky. These things I had to come to grips with to prove my fitness to represent all of the state. My House voting record, moreover, oriented to the consumers who predominate in a metropolitan area, was used effectively against me in the agricultural area of the state—a perfect case of the need to be close to all state problems.

Indispensable for the victor is public relations *savoir faire*—and this includes the whole field of public relations. It has become a lot more complex now than it once was. When I was a boy, a rather large stomach, a shad belly vest, a big cigar, and the ability to stand up and talk for two hours and a half seemed all that were necessary to stand a good chance of being elected Senator, governor, or, for that matter, any state-wide office. Today, with the development of electronics—radio and television—a candidate must have some know-how and ability in the use of each of the media. He has to have a certain amount of platform chemistry; he must be articulate, so that the audience can get a feel for what he is trying to say. He must be deft at fielding questions in a press conference—which can be devastating if he is not pretty fast on his feet—and he needs the ability to handle a microphone and to perform before television cameras.

Naturally, no one is equally adept at all of these. In running and planning a campaign, one emphasizes the particular method at which he is most proficient. I happen to be comfortable with the television question and answer program; someone else might not be, and should not use it. A part of public relations skill, then, is to know what you can and what you cannot do well.

Previous political experience helps, too. It can serve as a step toward the nomination besides being held up to the electorate as an indication of ability. For most members, the Senate is not their first elective office; they have arrived with a political background. Forty-two are former members of the House of Representatives. Twenty-one are ex-governors—in the Midwest and in less populated states the governorship is frequently a springboard to the Senate. In some instances Senators have served both as representative and governor. (In the House, incidentally, one member is a former governor and Senator.) Furthermore, we have four former lieutenant governors, three former Cabinet members and two ex-mayors. In addition, many have held lesser office at some time in their lives.

It is interesting to note that seven in the Senate are under forty years of age. I cannot recall a similar situation since the end of the Second World War. In all likelihood, there has not been such a percentage of young Senators since the early days of the Republic.

Turning from the qualities of the candidates to the campaign itself, there are several techniques and instruments that have been found useful, if not essential, in helping a candidate win office.

There is, of course, the tired old cliche that there is no substitute for work. The candidate cannot be lazy. His day is necessarily long in order to extend personal contact with as much of the electorate as humanly possible. After an evening speaking engagement and a fifty to one hundred-mile drive to the night's lodging, it is a joyless trial to arise at six in the morning to greet workers at a factory gate—especially when every third one explains with pithy profanity his low opinion of you. But there is more to a modern campaign than work of this sort.

The complexities of a political campaign state-wide in most of our states today have reached a level at which it is imperative that a candidate take a very searching survey or poll of his state, and that it be made by a competent professional. Most Senators or candidates for the Senate do not want to do this because they do not want to spend the money which, they think, could be better spent on advertisements, television time, and the like. But a survey in depth, in my opinion, is absolutely vital and essential.

It should be made early—in February or March of the election year—and followed up later. It does not have to cover too many people; a balanced sample can be worked out scientifically to permit you to cover very few. For example, in my 1962 campaign in Kentucky, where the population is roughly three million and the total vote cast roughly one million, we made only 600 interviews, but made them in a carefully-chosen cross-section of the Commonwealth. The probe should be deep; our interviews ran 55 minutes—and persons reveal a lot of what they are thinking in 55 minutes.

What does this do for you? If the survey is carefully and

professionally planned the candidate winds up with a good idea of the mind of the electorate. Most importantly, he uncovers his weaknesses. His opponent will do so eventually, but by then defenses will have been prepared. Also it spares him the awful shock of being caught off guard by the opposition's political blast. It saves him from defending himself unnecessarily against shots which are *not* hitting home with the electorate and lets him concentrate on issues which really could hurt him.

A concrete example of this occurred in my last campaign. I found through my survey that the question on which I was most vulnerable was my opposition to what was then the Kennedy Medicare Program. I had fought the program and fought it hard, and it was defeated in the Senate by 52 votes to 48. As it happened, one Senator who had voted against it said that he would have voted for it if his vote had been needed to pass it, so my opponent was able to say that Morton's vote killed medicare in that session. We discovered that this was my Achilles' heel. As a result, my staff insisted that in every talk or speech I made during the entire campaign (and in Kentucky you visit each one of the 120 counties) I had to give my reasons for my position. These reasons could be shown to be sound, in my opinion, and I gave them. I never got so tired as I did talking about medicare, but if I left it out of a speech my staff jumped me right away.

I spoke of this to a colleague who was running in a neighboring state and suggested that he do the same—I was certain that conditions in his state could not be that much different from mine—but he said, "I'm not going to say a word about medicare; my mail is 9 to 1 against medicare. I don't have to worry about it." And he was defeated. Of course his mail was 9 to 1 against medicare; it was coming from the doctors, the dentists, the nurses and the hospital superintendents and so forth. He wasn't hearing from the people. If he had taken a survey he would have heard from them and he might have come up with the same answers I did. But he was defeated, and in a very close election.

So the survey to me is (and was) vital. The poll reveals opposition weaknesses too. Protecting your own soft spots is only stemming the tide against you, but exploiting the opponent's vulnerability is raising the tide against him.

Although the poll is not taken to determine who is leading—

you will find out that on election night—it is useful to include such a question, because in the follow-up you can get a line on the progress of the campaign. If you are not progressing properly, the survey should show you what the trouble is. In general, however, there is no need to spend money just to see if you are gaining or losing. There are so many people today who take such polls and take them well—newspapers and others—that you can usually get that information free.

The quality of the candidate's organization can make or break him. It consists of financing, research, and a loyal personal following.

The financing phase should begin a year and a half before the campaign. This is essential because costs have grown so. In a state today of four or five million people, it is pretty hard to put on a decent Senate campaign for less than $500,000 or $600,000. All costs, but especially those for time on television and radio, and for newspaper advertisements, have skyrocketed. My 1962 campaign required about twice as much as the 1956 one and I did not do more in the second run than I had in the first—the prices had gone up. As Chairman of the Republican Senatorial Campaign Committee in the last election, I recommended to the chief aides of Republican Senators standing for re-election that their bosses report to me by April of 1965 who their finance chairmen would be for the 1966 campaign. By that time most of them did not know who their opponents would be, but I felt that it was essential for them to have their financial operations started.

Research results in the plan of the campaign. It brings out the issues and their development. And the first thing in research is a thorough study of your opponent from the day he was born to the present. If he has held office, everything he has said publicly, every decision he has made, everything he did in office must be studied. This may develop some weak spots in his armor.

The issues must be pared to those that interest your electorate— there is no use talking about the bracero program (the importation of labor from overseas or from Mexico) if it is of no interest to the people of your state. Too easily a candidate dwells on a question of particular interest to himself—something, in all likelihood, arising from his committee work that has little bearing on his state. Whatever may be a Senator's duties in the Senate itself, his people are concerned with their own problems at election time, and he should confine his campaign efforts to those issues. There are too many possible issues involved in an election for him to be effective if he spreads himself all over the map, shotgun style.

The candidate's personal following is vital. It does not replace the regular party organization, but very few candidates rely entirely on the regular organizations of their own states. They augment it. They cooperate, certainly, with it, and a few Senators are the leaders of the political organizations of their respective states—*de facto* leaders, of course, not State Chairmen. The late Senator Styles Bridges was "Mr. Republican" of New Hampshire, for example; he was a leader in his own state and in the United States Senate.

In most instances the Senator works with his party organization, but depends on a personal following whose first loyalty is to him. This protects him in the primary, for one thing. He is bound in the course of time to make some members of his party angry with him—he cannot make them all postmasters. The strong personal organization offsets the normal disaffection that develops in the party's ranks toward him as an individual. The case of Senator Walter George of Georgia illustrates this. Senator George was a great leader of the Senate—for many years Chairman of the Finance Committee and for many years Chairman of the Foreign Relations Committee. His work on those committees had been statesmanlike, but some of the legislation which had issued from his committees had brought him disfavor at home. When the 1956 elections approached he realized that his personal following had dwindled—he was by then quite an old man—and that he lacked the political strength to capture the primary in the face of his growing opposition. He simply decided not to run again.

In the South, and in some northern and prairie states where one-party government has prevailed until very recently, the primary was, of course, the only election in which there was a real fight. Even in a two-party state, however, a personal following may easily make the difference between victory and defeat. The most outstanding example of this was the personal organization built by Senator Hiram Fong in the 1964 election. He polled 53 per cent of the vote in his state, Hawaii, while the national ticket of his party only got 21 per cent. Beginning with a group of only three hundred people on whom he could rely utterly, he built up a total organization of 5,500 by election time. Each had a responsibility on election day to get so many voters to the polls. With this huge personal organization he was able to survive the Democratic landslide and to overcome the dissatisfaction of some members of his party—those who, for example, felt that he should have repudiated one of the labor unions which had supported him. The purpose of running for the Senate is to get elected to the Senate; that is the first purpose. You can worry about factions in your party after you get there.

Along with a personal following goes personal contact with the voters themselves. I think that Senator Proxmire of Wisconsin is probably an example of what it takes. When he was first elected to the Senate, it was the result of personal contact with literally tens of thousands of people—at factory gates, football games, or anywhere. He is a very hard worker, and he was working against tremendous odds to be elected.

Between campaigns it is very good to get home, renew contacts there, and make new ones. This precludes sitting behind the desk in your local office. It requires public appearances and plain handshaking. The people in some of the rural sections of this country—and this is especially true of the hill country of the Appalachian region—will not vote for anybody they have not actually met, except, of course, for the President and Vice President. As they say it in the mountains of my state, "I've never voted for a man 'less I've shook with him."

In summary, a successful campaign is based on four cornerstones. They are equally important. The first is the candidate—he must be articulate and obviously of Senate caliber. The second is issues—carefully selected and developed. The third is organization—the personal following supplemented by the regular party structure. Fourth is financing—and you start it early.

VI. The Relationship of a Senator to His Constituency

Senator Hugh Scott

A UNITED STATES SENATOR HAS MANY RESPONSIBILITIES AND duties. The demands on his time and his judgment are enormous. He never knows in the morning what will be faced during the day. But one thing is certain: Something will happen almost every day that has not happened before.

Perhaps this observation can best set the stage for a discussion of the relationship of a Senator to his constituency, because central to that relationship is the need for the Senator to maintain sufficient contact with his constituents to enable him to represent them properly in the numerous and often unanticipated decisions which he must make in their behalf.

A meaningful interchange of information and an interaction of ideas between a Senator and his constituents are basic to the legislative process, and constitute a bulwark of free government.

Probably the most difficult job facing a Senator is how to budget his time. I am an advocate of Congressional reform. I believe that in many instances we in the Congress are trying to cope with space-age problems under horse-and-buggy rules. I introduced a bill, which was incorporated by the Senate into the Legislative Reorganization Act of 1967, to enable the Legislative Reference Service of the Library of Congress to acquire automatic data processing facilities. With these facilities, Congress would be much better equipped to meet the growing research and informational requirements of legislation and of constituent requests for information.

RELATIONSHIP OF A SENATOR TO HIS CONSTITUENCY

A Senator represents the people of his State, the constituents who elected him. He has a much larger constituency as well. As a member of the group of 535 Congressmen and Senators who sit in the national legislature on Capitol Hill, he must be responsive to all the people of America.

In helping to shape legislation that determines what the national tax rate shall be, that affects the economy, and that regulates business and labor—to cite just a few instances—a Senator wields power that is felt far beyond the boundaries of his own State. A Senator's Constitutional responsibility to advise and consent on foreign policy means that his judgment, or his lack of it, will have repercussions well beyond our national borders.

But, the constituency which elects me—the people of Pennsylvania—commands my first attention. We carry on a continuing dialogue, which lets my constituently know what I am thinking and plays a very important part in helping me form my judgment on various matters.

Of course, no Senator simply "does the will" of the people who send him to Washington. There are too many "wills" to be done in any State. However, a constant check on the pulse of the State is indispensable in helping to form judgments. The attitude back home is not the only opinion maker, but it looms large in the making of decisions.

I listen to the same radio and television programs that every interested citizen tunes in. I read many magazines and newspapers from inside and outside my State.

But I also have other sources of information which are unique to a Senator. I often hear many of the "off-the-record" statements and opinions which shed more light on, or add emphasis to, the issues of the day. I am in daily contact with my colleagues in the Congress. I frequently meet with government officials, lobbying groups, and ambassadors in Washington. Often I am able to discuss world problems with visiting foreign dignitaries or newsmen. In addition, the many hearings and briefings, as well as the luncheons or official banquets, which are held in the nation's capital provide me with thorough and detailed information not available to many other citizens.

This is why I consider the communication between my constituents and myself a two-way street. I learn from my constituents.

They are among my most valuable teachers. But I have things to tell them. I must inform them of my actions, and the basis for them, so they know how they are being represented.

It is not always so clear, nor so easy to do.

Edmund Burke said, "Your representative owes you not his industry only but his judgement; and he betrays instead of serving you if he sacrifices it to your opinion."

When the U.S.-Soviet Consular Treaty was before the Senate for ratification, my office was besieged with mail opposed to the treaty. However, I felt compelled to vote in favor of ratification. I felt that the public had received much misleading information about that treaty. I explained why I favored the treaty, on the basis of information available to me, and pointed out the ways in which it would benefit the United States. I believe that most of my constituents understood my position, and I had many letters from people who had previously opposed the treaty saying that they had changed their opinion.

Most voters do not mark their ballot on the basis of how much was done for or against them or on who got what. They vote for the candidate they can trust to exercise good judgment. They do not all expect that a Senator's judgment will coincide with theirs 100 percent of the time, but they hope that over a period of time he will provide them with fair and reasonable representation.

That is one reason why the dialogue is so important. John Doe may be sputtering mad at me for the position I took last week, but if I keep him informed of all my positions, John Doe and I will find that we agree more often than not.

If a representative and his constituents do not work well together, both suffer, and the governmental process does not function as it should.

The general well-being of the body politic require responsive representation and an informed and interested public. If the public is apathetic, the representation usually becomes slothful.

People get the kind of government they deserve. If they are concerned about the quality of their government and alert to the caliber of their office-holders, then they will have good government. If people ignore what their government does and the way it functions, if the sum of their political involvement involves only marching to the polls on election day to decide between two candidates of whom they know little or nothing, then they will get lazy and inefficient government.

Government, somewhat like marriage, is something you have to work at to make successful. And politics is the way the private citizen involves himself in the processes of government. It is the responsibility of the elected officials to help keep this interest alive.

How do I go about establishing and maintaining this dialogue with my constituents? There is a very routine and practical system involved. The maintenance of the dialogue is the workaday concern of every member of a Senator's staff. Ninety percent of office operations is geared to this continuing dialogue.

Mail is one of the mainstays in this process of two-way communication. I receive an average of about 500 letters a day. When controversial legislation is before the Senate, or when some particularly crucial national or international issue is in the headlines, I receive as many as 3,000 letters in a single day.

All the mail is read, and all is answered, although the volume prevents me from answering each letter personally. I usually see about 50 to 60 letters each day. I dictate a great many of the answers myself, and carry on a continuous interchange with my staff on my positions and thoughts, thus enabling them to draft many replies.

The results of steady screening and evaluation of my mail serve as an indispensable indicator to me of the issues which concern my constituents, and the degree of their concern. My replies in turn keep them informed on my views and what I am doing.

Any constituent who takes the time and has the interest to write a letter deserves a reply. I receive every kind of letter imaginable—letters of concern, angry letters, letters of praise, letters requesting assistance, and an occasional hate letter. I sometimes learn that I have had babies, trees, or dogs named after me. One summer, a constituent asked me to find out when the rhododendrons were blooming in the Poconos. I was sorry to have to inform her that she had just missed the season.

One of the most inspiring letters, which I carried around in my pocket for a long time, was from a newly naturalized American citizen.

I had sent her a letter of congratulations, to which she replied:

". . . and you cannot imagine the feelings I experienced when I received your letter. How proud I am to be a citizen of a country where an important government official would take any notice of just a poor woman. This is the greatest time of my life, to live in such a free country. I will try always to be a good citizen and worthy of my great new country."

Many of the letters I receive require special attention and special assistance to individuals. These usually are from people who need help in cutting through the red tape of Federal bureaucracy. It may mean checking up on a request by a serviceman for compassionate leave, or trying to locate naturalization papers for an alien who cannot work until the processing has been completed.

I recently had my staff investigate a plea from some one whose much-needed Social Security check had been delayed for several months. Then there was another identical problem, and another. I discovered that the delays were caused by administrative tie-ups.

I discovered that it was a national problem and a severe one for Social Security recipients whose sole means of support are their monthly payments. The upshot of that first request for assistance was that I introduced a bill in the Senate, cosponsored by a number of other Senators, which would tighten up the administration of the Social Security system and provide means by which recipients could receive quick interim payments to avoid further delays.

I prepare a newsletter every month which goes to many thousand Pennsylvanians. It reports on legislation I have introduced, excerpts of my testimony before committees, and reports of other activities in the Senate of interest to my constituents.

The newsletter, in turn, inspires many letters from my constituents. Some people return the sheet with comments, most of which are interesting, some helpful in giving me ideas for new legislation, and a few colorfully critical of what I wrote.

One man wrote rather harsh comments in the margin beside every paragraph. I was tempted to take his name off my mailing list, but at the bottom of the page he wrote: "Dear Senator, thanks for sending me this newsletter every month."

I also prepare a monthly news column for daily and weekly newspapers in Pennsylvania.

The news media, of course, are among the most important channels of communication. My office puts out news releases almost daily which state my views and positions. They are sent to correspondents for Pennsylvania daily newspapers, news wire services, and radio and television stations. The news media representatives, in turn, often call on me to comment on developments in the news.

Every two weeks, when Congress is in session, I meet with Senator Joseph S. Clark, the Democratic Senator from Pennsylvania, to tape a half-hour television and radio program in the Senate Recording Studio in the basement of the Capitol Building. It is a unique continuing debate, the oldest program of its kind.

It provides an excellent forum for the two Senators from Pennsylvania. The program is carried by more than 57 radio and television stations in Pennsylvania, and is also seen and heard in bordering states. A typed transcript of the program is sent to the daily and weekly newspapers in the Commonwealth.

We try to have interesting guests. Among them have been Henry Cabot Lodge, John F. Kennedy, Edward Kennedy, Barry Goldwater, Everett McKinley Dirksen, and Hubert Humphrey, to mention only a few. Sometimes the guest is a radio or television personality, a spokesman for an urban slum improvement program, students, or other people of special interest to our viewers and listeners.

Our audience has seen, over nearly a decade, that Senator Clark and I agree on many issues, particularly in areas of concern to our Commonwealth. But we are often in sharp disagreement on how to bring about better government, on how various programs can most effectively be carried out, and especially on other matters dealing with our two political parties.

We usually get a pretty lively discussion going, and often a heated exchange will develop. One such exchange came during a discussion of the poverty program. Senator Clark was discussing a bipartisan committee formed in Philadelphia, ". . . to bring some sort of order out of a rather chaotic poverty situation."

> SCOTT: You have to call on Republicans to help bail you out.
> CLARK: Oh yes, there's no question about it. We like to keep the poverty program bipartisan and nonpartisan, Hugh, and I think you'll do better if you'll keep it bipartisan.

SCOTT: Well, I do, but I point out the best way to do that is to get able Republicans to bail out Democrats whenever they are in a mess.

CLARK: I think the worst reason in the world to support the poverty program on a long-range basis is the fear of the well-to-do that there may be riots in the streets. Good night, if we can't find more compassionate and better reasons for supporting the program than that, maybe we'd better get rid of it.

SCOTT: Joe, it isn't just the fear of the well-to-do. If there are riots and bloodshed in the streets, the people who get killed are people who are poor or disadvantaged, and they have more to fear than anybody else. The way to avoid riots and bloodshed, it seems to me, is to be fair with people and to keep your promises and if you appropriate money to be spent for them be sure it gets down to them.

Whenever either Senator Clark or I becomes a candidate for election, the program is discontinued for that campaign year.

Periodically—depending on my relationship to the major news of the day—I am invited to appear on network programs such as "Issues and Answers," "Youth Wants to Know," "Face the Nation," and others which reach a national audience.

More direct contact with my constituents comes through frequent trips to Pennsylvania for speaking engagements, and by speaking to visiting groups of constituents in Washington.

Each month, I receive from 100 to 250 invitations for speeches or attendance at various functions. Obviously, I cannot accept them all. When I cannot go, I often send a statement to be read, or I address the group over the telephone. Sometimes, members of my staff are able to fill speaking engagements in my behalf.

Through these regular trips to Pennsylvania, attendance at many functions both public and private, and a continuous stream of appointments and callers at my offices in Washington, Philadelphia, and Pittsburgh, I am able to keep in touch first hand with a large cross-section of my constituency.

These are the various ways which I use to maintain a dialogue with my constituents. Other Senators may use similar or entirely different means. But the goal is the same: the proper and effective functioning of our representative form of government.

Being a Senator is hard work, interesting work. I have yet to know a Senator who did not believe it to be the most challenging job in the world.

The Leadership and the Parties

Senators are not easily led, nor do political parties appear to be dominant factors in the Senate's deliberations and decisions. Lines are readily crossed and only rarely is the "great forum" used for debate on the issues dividing the national parties. Yet the basis of the Senate's organization is partisan; the man principally responsible for the scheduling of its legislative business is the Leader of the majority party. Agreements between party leaders facilitate the passage of much legislation—often by unanimous consent. Party-appointed objectors maintain vigil over their parties' interests on the Floor, and party is the most important single factor affecting how the members vote.

In late 1963 Majority Leader Mike Mansfield came under attack, some of it from members of his own party in the Senate, for the alleged weakness of his leadership and the failure of the Senate, under him, to act expeditiously on important legislation. His reply, which he had prepared shortly before the assassination of President John F. Kennedy on November 22, is reprinted here. (In the aftermath of the assassination he felt it inappropriate to make the speech, and simply inserted it into the Record instead.) His addendum, written for inclusion in this volume, carries the record of achievement through the 89th Congress.

The Republican record and the role or function of the minority are discussed by Senator Thomas H. Kuchel, Assistant Minority Leader. In his essay may be noted the admixture of cooperation and competition which the Senate rules compel the parties to maintain and which serves to abscure at times, as well as to make them share, the responsibility for success or failure of important legislation.

VII.   The Senate and its Leadership*

Senator Michael J. Mansfield

MR. PRESIDENT, SOME DAYS AGO BLUNT WORDS WERE SAID ON THE floor of the Senate. They dealt in critical fashion with the state of this institution. They dealt in critical fashion with the quality of the Majority Leadership and the Minority opposition. In doing so, a far more important matter than criticism or praise of the leadership was involved. It is a matter which goes to the fundamental nature of the Senate.

In this light, we have reason to be grateful because if what was stated was being said in the cloakrooms, then it should have been said on the floor. If, as was indicated, the functioning of the Senate itself is in question, the place to air that matter is on the floor of the Senate. We need no cloakroom commandos, operating behind the swinging doors of the two rooms at the rear, to spread the tidings. We need no whispered word passed from one to another and on to the press.

We are here to do the public's business. On the floor of the Senate, the public's business is conducted in full sight and hearing of the public. And it is here, not in the cloakrooms, that the Senator from Montana, the Majority Leader, if you wish, will address himself to the question of the present state of the Senate and its leadership. The Senator from Montana has nothing to conceal. He has nothing which is best whispered in the cloakrooms. What he has to say on this score will be said here. It will be said to all Senators and to all the members of the press who sit above us in more ways than one.

How, Mr. President, do you measure the performance of this Congress—any Congress? How do you measure the performance

* From the *Congressional Record,* November 27, 1963, pp. 22858–22862.

of a Senate of 100 independent men and women—any Senate? The question rarely arises at least until an election approaches. And, then, our concern may well be with our own individual performance and not necessarily with that of the Senate as a whole.

Yet that performance—the performance of the Senate as a whole—has been judged on the floor. Several Senators, at least, judged it and found it seriously wanting. And with the hue and cry thus raised, they found echoes outside the Senate. I do not criticize Senators for making the judgment, for raising the alarm. Even less do I criticize the press for spreading it. Senators were within their rights. And the press was not only within its rights but was performing a segment of its public duty which is to report what transpires here.

I, too, am within my rights, Mr. President, and I believe I am performing a duty of the leadership when I ask again: How do you judge the performance of this Congress—any Congress? Of this Senate—any Senate? Do you mix a concoction and drink it? And if you feel a sense of well-being thereafter decide it is not so bad a Congress after all? But if you feel somewhat ill or depressed then that, indeed, is proof unequivocal that the Congress is a bad Congress and the Senate is a bad Senate. Or do you shake your head back and forth negatively before a favored columnist when discussing the performance of this Senate? And if he, in turn, nods up and down, then that is proof that the performance is bad?

With all due respect, Mr. President, I searched the remarks of the Senators who have raised the questions. I searched them carefully for I do not make light of the criticism of any Member of this body. I searched them carefully for any insight as to how we might judge accurately the performance of this Senate, in order that we might try to improve it.

There is reference, to be sure, to time-wasting, to laziness, to absenteeism, to standing still and so forth. But who are the time-wasters in the Senate, Mr. President? Who is lazy? Who is an absentee? Each Member can make his own judgment of his individual performance. I make no apologies for mine. Nor will I sit in judgment on any other Member. On that score, each of us will answer to his own conscience, if not to his constituents.

But, Mr. President, insofar as the performance of the Senate as a whole is concerned, with all due respect, these comments on time-wasting have little relevance. Indeed, the Congress can, as it has—as it did in declaring World War II in less than a day—pass legislation which has the profoundest meaning for the entire nation. And by contrast, the Senate floor can look very busy day in and day out, month in and month out, while the Senate is, indeed, dawdling. At one time in the recollection of many of us, we debated a civil rights measure twenty-four hours a day for many days on end. We debated it shaven and unshaven. We debated it without ties, with hair awry and even in bedroom slippers. In the end, we wound up with compromise legislation. And it was not the fresh and well-rested opponents of the civil rights measure who were compelled to the compromise. It was, rather, the exhausted, sleep-starved quorum-confounded proponents who were only too happy to take it.

No, Mr. President, if we would estimate the performance of this Congress or any other, this Senate or any other, we will have to find a more reliable yardstick than whether, on the floor, we act as time-wasters or moonlighters. As every Member of the Senate and press knows, even if the public generally does not, the Senate is neither more nor less effective because the Senate is in session from 9:00 A.M. to 9:00 P.M. or to 9:00 A.M. the next day. In fact, such hours would most certainly make it less effective in present circumstances.*

Nor does the length of the session indicate a greater or lesser effectiveness. We live in a twelve-months nation. It may well be that the times are pushing us in the direction of a twelve-months Congress. In short, we cannot measure a Congress or a Senate by the standards of the stretch-out or of the speed-up. It will be of no avail to install a time-clock at the entrance to the Chamber for Senators to punch when they enter or leave the floor.

There has been a great deal said on this floor about featherbedding in certain industries. But if we want to see a featherbedding to end all featherbedding, we will have the Senate sit here day in and day out from dawn until dawn, whether or not

---

* One of the specific criticisms levied against the leadership had been its failure to increase the length of daily sessions or go into continuous session in order to expedite its business.—ED.

the calendar calls for it, in order to impress the boss—the American people—with our industriousness. We may not shuffle papers as bureaucrats are assumed to do when engaged in this art. What we are likely to shuffle is words—words to the President on how to execute the foreign policy or administer the domestic affairs of the nation. And when these words pall, we undoubtedly will turn to the Court to give that institution the benefit of our advice on its responsibilities. And if we run out of judicial wisdom we can always turn to advising the governors of the states or the mayors of the cities or the heads of other nations on how to manage their concerns.

Let me make it clear that Senators individually have every right to comment on whatever they wish and to do so on the floor of the Senate. Highly significant initiatives on all manner of public affairs have had their genesis in the remarks of individual Senators on the floor. But there is one clear-cut, day-in-and-day-out responsibility of the Senate as a whole. Beyond all others, it is the Constitutional responsibility to be here and to consider and to act in concert with the House on the legislative needs of the nation. And the effectiveness with which that responsibility is discharged cannot be measured by any reference to the clocks on the walls of the Chamber.

Nor can it be measured, really, by the output of legislation. For those who are computer-minded, however, the record shows that 12,656 bills and resolutions were introduced in the 79th Congress (1945–1946). And in the 87th Congress (1961–1962) 20,316 bills and resolutions were introduced, an increase of 60 percent. And the records show further that in the 79th Congress 2,117 bills and resolutions were passed and in the 87th 2,217 were passed.

But what do these figures tell us, Mr. President? Do they tell us that the Congress has been doing poorly because in the face of an 8,000 increase in the biannual imput of bills and resolutions the output of laws fifteen years later had increased by only a hundred? They tell us nothing of the kind.

If these figures tell us anything, they tell us that the pressures on Congress have intensified greatly. They suggest, further, that Congress may be resistant to these pressures. But whether Congress resists rightly or wrongly, to the benefit or detriment of the nation, these figures tell us nothing at all.

There is a refinement in the statistical approach. It may have more meaning than the gross figures in measuring the effectiveness of a Democratic administration. I refer to the approach which is commonly used these days of totaling the Presidential or Executive Branch requests for significant legislation and weighing against that total the number of Congressional responses in the form of law.

On this basis, if the Congress enacts a small percentage of the Executive Branch requests it is presumed, somewhat glibly and impertinently, to be an ineffective Congress. But if the percentage is high, it follows that it is classifiable as an effective Congress. I am not so sure that I would agree, and I am certain that the distinguished Minority Leader and his party would not agree that that is a valid test. The opposition might measure in precisely the opposite fashion. The opposition might, indeed, find a Democratic Congress which enacted little if any of a Democratic Administration's legislation, a paragon among Congresses. And yet I know that the distinguished Minority Leader does not reason in that fashion for he has acted time and again not to kill Administration measures but to help to pass them when he was persuaded that the interests of the nation so required.

In any event, the statistics on this score are not calculated to give aid and comfort to those who are in a hurry to mark off this Congress as a failure at the midway. For here, Mr. President, are the facts:

As of November 15, the Executive had submitted 125 legislative recommendations to the 88th Congress, in the form of messages, letters, and communications. In addition, fifteen appropriations bills have come down. Thus, the total is 140. For three of these measures, the Executive Branch has yet to suggest draft legislation. The working total of Executive requests, therefore is 137.

Of these measures, 45 have been enacted into law. Two have had conference reports filed and will shortly be enacted. In conference at the present time are six more. And already passed in the Senate and awaiting House action are 26 additional Executive measures. In sum, Mr. President, 79 of the requested 137 Executive measures, or 58 percent of the program, has, in effect, cleared the Senate. As a Democratic Senator who needs to make no apology to any Member on this side of the aisle for his voting record in support of the President, I, nevertheless, find nothing to brag about in these figures. But neither do I find any grounds for apology as Majority Leader. I ask any Member to search the *Record* and find in the postwar years, a basis for deprecating the work of the 88th Congress on a statistical basis of this kind. The 88th Congress has yet to run its course but about 60 percent at the midway is not in any sense an inadequate statistical response to the President's program. And I would point out that the figure of laws enacted pursuant to the President's program in the 87th Congress was 68 percent. And I ask the Senate to search the *Record* and find a basis for deprecating the work of that Congress on a statistical analysis of this kind.

In short, I see no basis for apology on statistical grounds either for this Congress to date or for the last. But at the same time, I do not take umbrage in statistics. I do not think that statistics, however refined, tell much of the story of whether or not a particular Congress or Senate is effective or ineffective.

But there is still another test which persuades me that the previous Congress under this Administration was and—before it is done in 1964—this Congress will be more than adequate. This test, admittedly, is a subjective one. Yet it may provide a more accurate insight than statistics into what really matters most in any Congress. I refer to the test of history. I refer to the capacity of a Congress—any Congress—to produce what might be called significant legislation of adjustment, legislation which is in consonance with the forces of change which are at work in the nation and in the world of its time. I refer to the capacity of a Congress to do its part, to do what it must, to keep the nation attuned to ever-changing national and international realities. I refer to the ability of a Congress to come to grips with those few specific critical issues which confront it and to act constructively on them.

And before it becomes fashionable to hold up to ridicule this Congress and the last as well, it seems to me appropriate to take a look at the historic record in the light of this criterion. It seems to me sensible to isolate from the appearance of things, from the hundreds of things which any Congress does, those few specific measures which past Congresses have enacted, measures which without too much stretch of the imagination may be regarded as significant legislation of adjustment—the legislation which reveals the vitality of a Congress in meeting the needs of the nation in its time.

[*The Majority Leader then listed the major measures passed by each of the Congresses from the 80th through the 86th Congress. He summarized as follows:*]

. . . The number of significant measures is not great in these pre-Kennedy Congresses. The range is from 7 or so in the two years of the 80th Congress to a high of 13 or so during the two years of the exceptional 85th Congress under the leadership of the distinguished Vice President, Mr. Johnson. For the most part, each two years witnessed the enactment of a total of eight or nine items and most of them elaborations or variations on themes already set in preceding years.

That is the record, Mr. President, of the Congresses from the end of World War II to the inception of the Kennedy Administration. When all else recedes into history, when the newspapers of the times yellow on the library shelves, when all years roll into the good old days, these are the measures, beyond the routine, which will count in terms of the shaping of the nation and of its place in the world. And it is largely on the basis of this legislation of adjustment that the historical judgments will be made. . . .*

We come now, Mr. President, to the record of the 87th Congress, the first Congress of the Kennedy Administration. Here, then, is the comparable list:

First. It passed the omnibus farm bill to reduce surpluses and to provide for a new land-use adjustment program.

Second. It authorized a program of health aid for migrant farm workers.

Third. It extended unemployment benefits an additional 13 weeks.

---

* In the original, the material in this paragraph came at the beginning of the one immediately preceding it. The editorial inversion of these two portions has been made in order to retain their continuity of the Statement despite the omission of the detailed lists of measures passed by the earlier Congresses—ED.

Fourth. It provided a program of aid to dependent children of the unemployed.

Fifth. It increased minimum wages from $1.00 to $1.25 and extended coverage to several million additional workers.

Sixth. It established the Area Redevelopment Program.

Seventh. It increased old-age insurance benefits and provided for retirement of men at 62 and liberalized disability payments.

Eighth. It authorized almost $5 billion in new funds under the Omnibus Housing Act.

Ninth. It extended the efforts to control water pollution.

Tenth. It established the Manpower Training program.

Eleventh. It accelerated the public works program by an authorization of $900 million.

Twelfth. It made a significant revision in the tax structure.

Thirteenth. It authorized direct loans for housing for the elderly.

Fourteenth. It provided for voluntary pensions plans under the tax laws.

Fifteenth. It enacted the trade expansion program.

Sixteenth. It passed the communications satellite bill.

Seventeenth. It established the Peace Corps.

Eighteenth. It established the U.S. Arms Control and Disarmament Agency.

Nineteenth. It created the U.S. Travel Service.

Twentieth. It authorized the purchase of U.N. bonds to save that organization from bankruptcy.

Twenty-first. It initiated a Federal program on juvenile delinquency.

Twenty-second. It provided a program of aid for educational TV in the schools and colleges.

Twenty-third. It ratified the Treaty of the Organization for Economic Cooperation and Development.

Twenty-fourth. It approved a constitutional amendment abolishing the poll tax.

Twenty-fifth. It passed a substantial aid bill.

Twenty-sixth. The Senate invoked cloture for the first time in several decades.

Mr. President, I will not draw comparisons between the 87th Congress and those which preceded it. Each Congress has its own challenges. Each does the best it can. But I will say to every Member of this body, this is the record that counts most. This is the record which you made. It is not the record of the Majority Leader or the Minority Leader. It is the Senate's record and as the Senator from Montana, I, for one, will not make light of these achievements in the first two years of the Kennedy Administration. And the achievement is no less because the 87th Congress did not meet at all hours of the night, because it rarely titillated the galleries, or because it failed to impress the visiting newsmen and columnists.

And now, Mr. President, we come to the 88th Congress and particularly to this Senate. We come to this Senate which some have already consigned to the wasteheaps of history. We come to its leadership which some find is to be pitied if, indeed, it is not to be scorned.

Here, Mr. President, I will include in the list—in the list of the significant legislation of adjustment—not only those measures which have cleared the Congress but also items which have at least cleared the Senate and are awaiting final action. Congress is not for one year. It is for two. What this Congress will in the end produce we cannot say until this Congress comes to an end some time in 1964. But to date in this Congress and in this Senate, here is the list:

First. It has initiated a program which begins to recognize the full dimensions of major health problems of the nation and to come to grips with them—mental illness and mental retardation.

Second. It has expanded Federal aid for maternal and child-health services and for crippled children.

Third. It has acted to forestall what would otherwise have been a crippling railroad shutdown.

Fourth. It has acted to provide for a vast expansion in training and research facilities in medicine, dentistry, and related sciences.

Fifth. It has acted to expand academic facilities in higher education through grants and loans for construction.

Sixth. It has acted to expand vocational education and extended for three years the National Defense Education Act and the impacted areas program.

Seventh. It has acted on the problem of mass transit.

Eighth. It has acted to establish a Domestic Peace Corps.

Ninth. It has acted to establish a system of Federal public defenders.

Tenth. It has acted to create a Youth Conservation Corps.

Eleventh. It has acted on a water resources research program.

Twelfth. It has acted to preserve wilderness areas.

Thirteenth. It has acted to expand the area redevelopment program.

Fourteenth. It has acted on the problems of air and water pollution.

Fifteenth. It has authorized a substantial foreign aid program.

Sixteenth. It has given consent to the ratification of the nuclear test ban treaty.

That is the record, Mr. President, at the halfway mark in the 88th Congress. And once again I will leave it to others who are so inclined to draw comparisons with past Congresses. But I will say that no Senator need be ashamed of this record. The record is no less a record because it has taken ten months of work to achieve. It is no less a record because it has been produced by cooperation, because the leadership wields no whip and seeks no whip to wield. And the record is for one year not for the two to which every Congress is entitled.

However this midway Congress may compare with what has gone before, the leadership would be the first to recognize that there are inadequacies in it. And the most serious, in my judgment, are neither the status of the civil rights bill nor the tax bill. The most serious, in my judgment, have to do with the day-to-day financial housekeeping of the government. We have got to face the fact that if we are going to have an orderly fiscal administration of this government we cannot long continue with the practice of raising every few months, as a ritual, the legal debt ceiling. Nor can we expect a rational administration of the vast and far-flung activities of the Executive Branch of this government if the basic appropriations bills do not become law until months after the fiscal year begins.

I do not know where the answer to these problems lies. I do not blame the House and I most certainly cannot blame the Senate which must await the completion of House action on legislation of this type before considering it. And how the Senate is going to discharge its constitutional responsibilites on appropriations bills by July 1, the beginning of the fiscal year, when some of the bills do not reach the Senate until long after June 30, I do not know. This year, for example, the District of Columbia appropriations arrived in the Senate Committee on July 15. The military construction appropriation has just arrived. And the foreign aid appropriation has not even yet started its journey to the Senate.

I want to say again that I do not place the responsibility for this breakdown on the House, and even less do I place it on the Senate Appropriations Committee.

Whatever the causes, and they are varied, the problem is still there. It has been growing worse over the years and if it is not faced soon, it will be a standing invitation to national financial chaos. Perhaps, what the distinguished Senator from Georgia [Mr. Russell] has suggested on occasion, along the lines of dividing the initiative on appropriations measures between the House and Senate may provide at least a partial solution. Perhaps, what the distinguished Senator from Washington [Mr. Magnuson] has proposed in the way of a division of the Congressional year between a legislative and an appropriating session may be helpful. Or perhaps the problem is even more fundamental. Perhaps, it is the persistance of the illusion of a seven months Congress in a twelve-months nation which is at the root of the difficulty and with this illusion, the incongruity of a June 30 fiscal closing in a December 31 government and nation.

Whatever the difficulty, we are and have been for some years, I repeat, on a course of increasing disorderliness in the management of the fundamental fiscal affairs of the government. I, for one, would welcome an initiative from the Administration and the relevant Committees looking to the establishment of a special Commission to explore this problem and to come up with recommendations for its solution. The job needs to be done and it needs to be done quickly.

If the Senate is not wholly at fault with regard to the appropriations situation, neither is it wholly at fault with regard to such measures as Health care and the Tax bill. . . .

Here again, Mr. President, as in the case of appropriations, we have got to face the fact that the Congress, under the Constitution and its established procedures is not basically equipped to respond, to reach a decision one way or another, on urgent matters which go to the heart of our national economic structure. And in all honesty, we have got to face the fact that in this instance, a failure to respond with some degree of urgency to an urgent Presidential request consigns to the Congress—to the whole Congress—a great responsibility for whatever consequences flow to the nation from this failure. . . .

I turn, finally, to the recent criticism which has been raised as to the quality of the leadership. I do not question the right of anyone to raise this question—certainly not the right of the Senate and the press, to do so. I regard every Member with respect and esteem and every Member in his own way has reciprocated that sentiment, and I am sure that no Member intends to do me ill. As for the press, it has been invariably fair, even kind, in its treatment of me personally. I have never been misquoted on any remarks I have made in the Senate and only on rare occasions have I been misinterpreted and, even then, understandably so.

Of late, Mr. President, the descriptions of the Majority Leader, of the Senator from Montana, have ranged from a benign Mr. Chips, to glamourless, to "tragic mistake." I have not yet seen "wet-nurse of the Senate" but that, too, may not be long in coming.

It is true, Mr. President, that I have taught school, although I cannot claim either the tenderness, the understanding, or the perception of Mr. Chips for his charges. I confess freely to a lack of glamour. As for being a "tragic mistake," if that means, Mr. President, that I am neither a circus ring-master, the master of ceremonies of a Senate night club, a tamer of Senate lions, or a wheeler and dealer, then I must accept, too, that title. Indeed, I must accept it, if I am expected as Majority Leader to be anything other than myself—a Senator from Montana who has had the good fortune to be trusted by his people for over two decades and done the best he knows how to represent them, and to do what he believes to be right for the nation.

Insofar as I am personally concerned, these or any other labels can be borne. I achieved the height of my political ambitions when I was elected Senator from Montana. When the Senate saw fit to designate me as Majority Leader, it was the Senate's choice not mine and what the Senate has bestowed, it is always at liberty to revoke.

But so long as I have this responsibility, it will be discharged to the best of my ability by me as I am. I would not, even if I could, presume to a tough-mindedness which, with all due respect to those who use this cliche, I have always had difficulty in distinguishing from soft-headedness or simple-mindedness. I shall not don any Mandarin's robes or any skin other than that to which I am accustomed in order that I may look like a Majority Leader or sound like a Majority Leader—however a Majority Leader is supposed to look or sound. I am what I am and no title, political face-lifter, or image-maker can alter it.

I believe that I am, as are most Senators, an ordinary American with a normal complement of vices and, I hope, virtues, of weaknesses and, I hope, strengths. As such, I do my best to be courteous, decent, and understanding of others and sometimes fail at it. But it is for the Senate to decide whether these characteristics are incompatible with the Leadership.

I have tried to treat others as I would like to be treated and almost invariably have been. And it is for the Senate to decide, too, whether that characteristic is incompatible with the Senate Leadership.

I have done my best to serve the people whom I represent and, at the same time, to exercise such independent judgment as I may have as to what is best for the nation as a whole, on national and international issues. If that is incompatible with the Senate leadership that, too, is for the Senate to decide.

I have always felt that the President of the United States—whoever he may be—is entitled to the dignity of his office and is worthy of the respect of the Senate. I have always felt that he bears a greater burden of responsibility than any individual Senator for the welfare and security of the nation. For he alone can speak for the nation abroad, and he alone, at home, stands with the Congress as a whole, as constituted representatives of the entire American people. In the exercise of his grave responsibilies, I believe we have a profound responsibility to give him whatever understanding and support we can, in good conscience and in conformity with our independent duties. I believe we owe it to the nation of which all our states are a part—particularly in matters of foreign relations—to give to him not only responsible opposition but responsible cooperation. If these concepts, too, are incompatible with the Majority Leadership, then that, too, is for the Senate to decide.

And, finally, within this body I believe that every Member ought to be equal in fact no less than in theory, that they have a primary responsibility to the people whom they represent to face the legislative issues of the nation. And to the extent that the Senate may be inadequate in this connection, the remedy lies not in the seeking of short-cuts, not in the cracking of nonexistent whips, not in wheeling and dealing, but in an honest facing of the situation and a resolution of it by the Senate itself, by accommodation, by respect for one another, by mutual restraint and, as necessary, adjustments in the procedures of this body.

I have been charged with lecturing the Senate. And perhaps these remarks will also be interpreted in this fashion. But all I have tried to do is state the facts on this institution as I see them. The Constitutional authority and responsibility does not lie with the leadership. It lies with all of us individually, collectively, and equally. And in the last analysis, deviations from that principle must in the end act to the detriment of the institution. And, in the end, that principle cannot be made to prevail by rules. It can prevail only if there is a high degree of accommodation, mutual restraint and a measure of courage—in spite of our weaknesses— in all of us. It can prevail only, if we recognize that, in the end, it is not the Senators as individuals who are of fundamental importance. In the end, it is the institution of the Senate. It is the Senate itself as one of the foundations of the Constitution. It is the Senate as one of the rocks of the Republic.

ADDENDUM

Subsequent to the above statement of November 27, 1963 and the tragic death of President Kennedy, the Congress remained in session throughout the year, approving an authorization of $3.6 billion for foreign aid and appropriating $3 billion for fiscal 1964. In addition, it continued the Peace Corps, and completed action on a controversial river basins authorization.

Among the most important actions of the first session of the 88th Congress were the three new education programs—medical school aid, college aid, and vocational education—to which reference was made, plus the impacted areas and National Defense Education Act extensions and federal aid to public libraries. In addition there was enacted a "bold new approach" to mental illness and retardation.

When the 88th Congress adjourned October 3, 1964, it had compiled an extraordinary record in terms of the sheer volume of significant legislation. Included among the measures which were enacted was the Civil Rights Act of 1964 which was passed in the Senate after 75 days of discussion and the invocation of cloture.

In a salute to this Congress, President Johnson said it had "enacted more major legislation, met more national needs, disposed of more national issues than any other session of the century or the last."

Then came the 89th Congress, which was described as the "greatest in American history." It was the Congress which—

Established mandatory Federal standards for auto safety;
Authorized the Highway safety program;
Established a new Cabinet-level Department of Transportation;
Authorized the Highway beautification program;
Charted the course for Federal aid to education;
Approved for the first time in U.S. history, Federal scholarships for undergraduate college students;
Established the National Teachers Corps;
Expanded the National School Lunch Act to include a 2-year child nutrition program;
Established the National Technical Institute to provide higher education for the deaf;
Enacted the International Education Act;
Provided Medicare for the aged;
Provided a 7 percent increase for social security beneficiaries;
Enacted the Drug Abuse Control Act;
Enacted the rent supplement program;
Established the Older American Act to provide grants for developing programs for the aged;
Authorized a 3-year program of grants to establish an estimated 25 regional medical programs to research such diseases as heart, cancer, and stroke;

Enacted the Cigarette Labeling bill to warn the public of the possible dangers of cigarette smoking;
Enacted the Voting Rights Act;
Eliminated the national origins quota system in immigration;
Enacted the Truth in Packaging Act;
Established the new city demonstration program;
Created the new Cabinet Department of Housing and Urban Development;
Increased the minimum wage; and
Provided for Presidential continuity.

VIII. The Role of the Senate Minority

Senator Thomas H. Kuchel

OUR NATION HAS THRIVED ON THE CONCEPT OF PEACEFUL competition among the ideas and produce of men in the open market place. Our historic two-party system is a clear political reflection of this American tradition. It provides for the necessary clash of ideas, the discussion and disagreement, the controversy and, finally, the compromise which makes progress possible.

Any vital institution must be prepared for change. That is an irresistable law of life. In the modern world we have heard much of the concept of change by "revolution." The wake of bloodshed left by this much-abused concept in many emerging nations has underscored, by contrast, the value of our own system of peaceful exchange of power from one political party to the other. This is the critical asset of a representative political system.

Every society must learn to move with the times or it becomes moribund. President Eisenhower said in his Second Inaugural Address:

> Across all the globe there harshly blow the winds of change. And we—though fortunate be our lot—know that we can never turn our backs on them.

Historically, any party which has become too doctrinaire or has tried to impose a loyalty oath on its members has simply withered away. Party loyalty is a voluntary matter. The party which has accommodated to a variety of challenging ideas in a manner permitting it to contend peacefully against the other has been able to win the faith of the people.

This spirit has molded both parties in the United States Senate, where I am proud to represent the people of California. The competition is hard, but it follows the basic ground rules of decency and fair play. It permits a peaceful reversal of roles between majority and minority. It keeps alive for the minority the hope that it will become the governing party by proving to the voters what it considers the better wisdom and virtue of its own views. It allows for a loyal opposition and for overall cooperation among all Americans in times when national unity is needed.

The Senate, as an institution, is peculiarly designed to give effect to the activities of the minority party. The rules and traditions of the Senate provide a congenial atmosphere for opposing ideas. The tradition of individual debate has provided an excellent outlet for minority views.

This has been particularly true in recent years when the Republican party has been relatively weak in terms of the number of seats it holds. The Senate provides an effective forum for criticism of Administration policies. The longer terms of Senators allow them to look beyond the immediate cut and thrust of transient political battles and to formulate the principal themes which the party requires to meet its national responsibilities.

The Republicans in the Senate are not a party unto themselves, but part of a broader organization seeking to discharge its responsibilities to, and acquire support from, the public. They are part of a political organization which competes to win local contests in many states, to control the majority in state legislatures, to win governorships, to gain a majority in the Congress, and to compete for the highest political office of all, the Presidency. The tension created by the two-party system in the United States forces into the foreground the basic goal of the minority party—to demonstrate that it deserves to become the majority, and take over the reins of national administration.

This requires a point of view far broader than the activities of the Senate itself. It demands an enormous effort at coordination of policy.

Except in rare circumstances, the members of the majority party in control of Congress have at their disposal the resources of the Presidency and the Executive administration. It controls an immense apparatus of power and publicity. Only through the most determined efforts of communication can nationwide appreciation of the accomplishments of the minority ever be achieved.

The minority party cannot rest content with mere self-laudatory remarks on the floor of the House or Senate. Its members must move out among the people themselves both to hear the concerns of the people and to make them aware of the response by the minority.

The national press will frequently amplify one party's work, particularly when the legislative record is unmistakable. In 1964 and 1965, the Republican minority in the Senate played the commanding role in the enactment of civil rights legislation. On this issue, the opposition within the majority party was bitter and entrenched. Without the careful and tenacious effort of the Republican minority leadership, no legislation of consequence could ever have been passed. The offices of the minority leaders became, quite literally, the study and drafting center from which the bills emerged which thereafter became law. It was clear where the credit lay for this accomplishment, and the press gave due recognition.

But the minority is not always so fortunate. In 1962, the Administration's Manpower Development and Training Act was moribund in the House. The obituaries were already in print. Revitalized and rewritten by House and Senate Republicans, an acceptable program was finally enacted into law. Yet, the majority party claimed the credit, and continues to do so today.

To assure that the activity of the minority in the national legislature is understood throughout the nation, a number of institutions have been created to bring the work of the party more into focus at all levels of the Republican organization. The minority leaders in the Senate and the House have formed the Joint Leadership Committee to provide a point of vantage of comment on the issues of the day and to present policy statements on behalf of the party's legislative leadership. This Committee puts forward the formal "State of the Union" message presented by the minority at the beginning of each session of the Congress.

After the 1964 defeat another institution, the Republican Coordinating Committee, was constituted, with solid support from all segments of the party, to provide for regular meetings of party leaders from every level of government and private activity throughout the country. Their efforts are thoroughly coordinated with the activities of the party in the Senate and the House of

Representatives. The Coordinating Committee provides for consultation on critical issues and a steady publication of views by its various task forces.

In all of this, the minority's activities in the Senate play a vital role.

Whether in majority or minority, Senate Republicans have for over twenty years maintained a broad gauge leadership organization. At the beginning of each session, all Republican Senators, acting in a body, elect a Conference Chairman and Secretary, Minority Leader and an Assistant Leader, known as the "Whip," and a Chairman of the Policy Committee. These five comprise the Republican Senate leadership. In addition, a Senatorial Campaign Committee Chairman and Assistant, a Committee on Committees Chairman, a Personnel Committee Chairman, and a Calendar Committee Chairman are selected. Individual Senators are assigned to each of these committees. There is no attempt to concentrate the leadership's offices in the hands of one or two Senators.

The minority holds a weekly policy meeting attended by all Republican Senators. It is the occasion for briefings by the leadership, informal discussion, and, at relatively rare times, for decisions by the Policy Committee or Conference. In addition to our numerous standing committee meetings, and our separate individual conferences on legislative substance and strategy, the minority has a regular opportunity to meet en bloc. It has proven a highly useful means of communication because of its open informality, particularly in the case of our weekly luncheons. I have often wondered why my Senate brethren on the Democratic side don't have such weekly meetings.

The role of the minority in the Senate is different for Republicans than for Democrats. Ours is a party of considerable ideological homogeneity. In the 85 key votes that were taken in the first half of 1967, Republicans were unanimous on 19 of them, the Democrats only on three. There is a strong tradition based on our fundamental views regarding human liberty, individual initiative, free competitive enterprise, and a sound husbanding and conservation of resources. Our party tends not to represent special groups, classes, or elements, but rather makes a broad appeal throughout the country based on this point of view. Ours is a party founded essentially on the American dream as broadly understood since the time of Abraham Lincoln. Our scope is, or tends to be, national, rather than sectional. These are basic concepts of democracy. Some regard them as "liberal." Others may call them "conservative." They are, in my view, a matter of fulfilling the needs of the people.

The Republican minority in the Senate has been able to record an impressive list of activities and achievements. I would divide these into four general categories.

First is the necessary duty of constructive opposition. A basic tenet of the Republican point of view is a responsible fiscal policy which demands demonstration of the public interest before justifying any expenditure and which seeks to control expenditures generally in a manner consistent with a growing economy and a sound employment policy. A common sense approach to the Federal budget together with a clear set of public priorities is the essence of this idea.

In 1966, when the Republican leadership discovered that funds were already available to support certain aspects of the foreign aid program through the next fiscal year, Senator Dirksen—speaking for the minority—moved for an appropriate cut in the foreign aid authorization. This was supported by the Senate as a whole.

In 1967, the Republican party has been nearly unanimous in its objection to the Federal campaign fund financing program supported by the Administration. The party as a whole, I believe, rejects the view that the Federal Government has a role to play in centralizing and directing funds to political campaigns of state and local organizations. Indeed, it is the vitality of these groups which provide the necessary counterweight to Federal power.

Second is the sponsorship of constructive alternatives. The Republican party is particularly interested in fostering individual initiative. Often Administration spending programs have been successfully countered by Republican proposals to encourage private enterprise through tax reductions. In the last Congress, Senators Cooper and Carlson proposed bills to provide for encouragement of anti-pollution programs by this mechanism. In the 89th Congress and again in the 90th Congress, a large number of Republicans joined in sponsoring the proposed "Human Investment Act" to provide tax incentives to encourage industry to establish special job training programs to alleviate the twin evils of unemployment and limited opportunity resulting from curtailed education.

The Republican party has come forward with constructive suggestions for the peaceful settlement of labor disputes affecting the public interest. The Administration has promised that proposals would be forthcoming to provide means to settle major disputes, such as the recent rail strike, and the 1966 New York transit strike, both of which affected the public consumer, in a total context, perhaps as much or more than management and labor. This is a critical national problem, but, regrettably, no proposal for a long term solution to these recurring issues was forthcoming from the Administration in time to aid in settlement of the 1967 rail strike.

Third are legislative accomplishments proposed by the minority which have found acceptance in the Congress as a whole. I have earlier mentioned the Civil Rights Act of 1964, the Voting Rights Act of 1965, and the Manpower Development and Training Act, which were largely the product of the Republican minority. It is also fair to say that there would be no Medicare bill in this country were it not for the progressive proposals of some Senate Republicans whose views ultimately were accepted by the late President Kennedy. It was this effort which paved the way to bringing into the Medicare program participation by private health programs and which encouraged a sound actuarial basis for its administration.

When I first came to the Senate 15 years ago, the Republican party had a majority of one vote. Regrettably, that position eroded over the years until the party held barely one-third of the seats. Today the trend has been reversed with the arrival of five new men to begin to rebuild our ranks. Those five, Senators Hatfield, Percy, Brooke, Baker, and Hansen, are stars who will be a credit to their country and to their party as well.

It is in the public interest for the opposition to demonstrate its vigor both in logic and in votes. It is not good that two-thirds of the Senate be members of one party. The Republican minority has played a vital role in checking excesses, in seeking to control spending, and in spearheading the use of free competitive enterprise in social development. Thus, in 1966 the Senate adopted my own amendment to the laws governing the Poverty Program. This measure gave preference to the use of free competitive enterprise in alleviating the burdens of suffering and providing a new horizon of opportunity for the disadvantaged segment of our nation. It was ultimately accepted with substantial Democratic support.

Last year the Congress of the United States finally recognized the fundamental inequity of treating workers in agriculture less favorably than those in industry. The national minimum wage law for agriculture was a proposal which I had repeatedly introduced in the Senate, with the official support of the Republican party in California. The bill which was passed in 1966 by the Congress was essentially this proposal.

It is fair to say that there would not have been a Consular Treaty with the Soviet Union in 1967 were it not for the overwhelming support of Republicans and particularly of the Republican leadership. The minority joined to overcome a major assault on this international agreement which had its roots in the proposals of the Eisenhower Administration, and which bore General Eisenhower's earnest approval.

Fourth is the area of necessary bipartisanship. Since the time of Arthur Vandenberg, the United States of America has based its foreign policy on a broad range of national support. The actions of our Presidents, whether Republican or Democrat, have been based on a bipartisan approach to America's role in the world. It is necessary that our nation be united in the face of the seemingly never-ending crises erupting throughout the world. The Republican party has supported the American effort in resistance to aggression in Vietnam. It has maintained firm support of the Atlantic Alliance and of a strong policy of good will and partnership with the American republics of the Western Hemisphere.

Beyond foreign policy, there are other areas where bipartisanship is essential. It is particularly necessary when any measure requiring a two-thirds vote comes before the Senate, for example, in the ratification of treaties or the breaking of a filibuster. The present rules of the Senate call for a two-thirds majority of those present and voting to put an end to the rule of unlimited debate. Bipartisan cooperation is necessary to overcome endless talkathons. And they occur, believe it or not, on a wide gamut of legislative proposals, always by a small group who know they don't have enough votes to prevail, so they decide to talk the proposal to death.

Bipartisanship is necessary in any area where the rules of the Senate are involved. Thus, Republicans have joined with members on the other side of the aisle in proposing a bill to provide for disclosure of the assets of Members of Congress, their key staff members, Congressional candidates, and ranking members of the Executive Branch on an annual basis. We believe that such legislation is in the public interest.

I have listed a broad range of achievement of the minority party. It is true that without votes legislation cannot be passed. The minority party through the continued pressure which it brings to bear can keep the majority party responsible to the public will. The minority party, by anticipating issues and preparing its own legislative solutions, can seek public approval and force the majority to take action, even if support for its own measures fail to pass. It is this ability to innovate and come forward with new and dynamic proposals which keep the American body politic healthy. It is true of Republicans and Democrats alike that a good proposal will meet support from both parties. My esteemed colleague, the Dean of Senate Republications, George Aiken of Vermont, recently made the point:

> As Republicans, let us not be afraid of the "me, too" charge which is sometimes levied against us. If a Democrat says we need better health, I am not going to come out for poorer health just to disagree with him.

All responsible Republicans recognize the wisdom of his point of view. This mechanism works both ways—whoever comes up with the best approach to a modern problem will ultimately win support in the Senate—and at the polls.

The Republican party in the Senate plays a vital role in keeping alive the possibility of change in the national Administration. Its role is to provide the counterweight in the delicate mechanism of our national political life, insuring that when the majority has spent its force there will be another element waiting and ready to keep the nation moving.

On the Senate Floor

At some point in a volume such as this, the Senate ought to be allowed to speak for itself. In these excerpts from the debate on rules which opened the First Session of the 86th Congress, the Senate speaks not only for, but about itself and its place in the American political system.

Amendments to several rules were proposed, but the central attack was upon the Senate's most distinctive instrument of negative power, the filibuster. The rules of the Senate do not provide for the filibuster as such. Rather, the filibuster is made possible because Rule XXII, the rule which contains the provision for cloture (shutting off debate), requires a two-thirds majority for the purpose and is in other respects so difficult to apply that, in addition to the votes, substantial determination and, usually, the assistance of the leadership are required to implement it. (Additionally, Rule XIX, which Senator Morse cited at the beginning of his filibuster on p. 105, permits an individual Senator to speak as long as he wishes during his first speech on a question. This provides an opportunity to filibuster, but one limited to the physical endurance of the Senator seeking to utilize it.)

The attack came from a group commonly referred to as "Senate Liberals," but more specifically one which saw the filibuster as the chief obstacle to effective civil rights legislation. As frequently happens in the Senate, the route to substantive legislation required an assault first upon the procedural barriers to action. The underlying issue was recognized by all concerned, but came to the surface only occasionally, with apparently neither side willing to risk a direct test on it at this point.

The strategy was complex. Aware of a pending attack on Rule XXII, Majority Leader Lyndon B. Johnson introduced Senate Resolution 5 (p. 89), which offered a slight relaxation of the rule—a relaxation apparently calculated to command majority support against the more radical reform element.* His resolution also, however, was de-

---

* It has also been suggested that Presidential ambitions were involved. Vice President Richard M. Nixon, who was to become the Republican candidate in 1960, had issued an informal advisory opinion two years earlier *signed to forestall future attacks on the rules by providing that they be continuous from Congress to Congress thereafter.*

Countering this, Senator Clinton P. Anderson of New Mexico introduced his substitute (p. 90), which declared that in any new Congress the Senate should adopt its rules de novo. *The substitute, according to the normal rules of parliamentary procedure, was debated first and, because it raised impressive Constitutional questions about the nature of the Senate, produced the self-examination which makes up the bulk of the material reproduced here.*

When the substitute had been put to a vote and defeated, the liberal forces then tested the accuracy of Senator Johnson's calculation of the mood of the Senate by offering a series of amendments differing from his largely in terms of the size of the majority which should be required to impose cloture—simple majority, three-fifths, etc. (The debate and votes on these amendments are not shown in the excerpts.) Johnson's position having held, the original resolution finally passed.

In the selections from the debate given here, an attempt has been made to show various moods and styles as well as some of the parliamentary maneuvering characteristic of Senate Floor action, but excerpts cannot present an accurate picture in at least one respect. Inevitably the leisurely tone—the repetitiousness and, at times, the dullness—is lost. Colloquies become crisper and rambling addresses succinct. The passages on these pages would occupy less than ten pages of the Congressional Record, *a length exceeded by each of several senators in their individual speeches.*

---

which opened the way for the present assault to the rule—an action regarded as giving him a liberal image. Johnson, who contested with John F. Kennedy for the Democratic nomination in 1960 and became his Vice President and later, President, might have seen some advantage in gaining for himself also a record of favoring relaxation of the Rule.

IX. The Debate on Senate Rules Change, 1959*

Thursday, January 8, 1959

THE SENATE MET AT 10 O'CLOCK A.M.

The Chaplain, Rev. Frederick Brown Harris, D.D., offered the following prayer:

Eternal God, Father of all men, who putteth down the mighty from their seats and exalteth the humble and the meek, without whom life has no spiritual source, no meaning above the dust on which we tread, but with whom there is power for the present and hope for the future; in this day of destiny, we seek Thee as our fathers have sought Thee in every generation, when the problems they faced were as frowning heights before their climbing feet. In this high and solemn chamber of debate and decision, may the great causes that concern Thy human family, the selfless ministries that help to heal the open sores of the world, gain the utter allegiance of our labor and our love, as we march with fearless tread in the gathering armies of friendship whose armor is the shield of Thy truth and whose sword is the invincible might of Thy love, against which all the spears of hate cannot ultimately prevail. We ask it in the dear Redeemer's name. Amen.

THE JOURNAL

On request of Mr. Johnson of Texas, and by unanimous consent, the reading of the Journal of the proceedings of Wednesday, January 7, 1959, was dispensed with....

---

* *Congressional Record,* January 8–12, 1959. pp, S63–S476.

MESSAGE FROM THE HOUSE

A message from the House of Representatives, by Mr. Bartlett, one of its reading clerks, informed the Senate that a quorum of the House of Representatives had assembled; that Honorable Sam Rayburn, a Representative from the State of Texas, had been elected Speaker; and Ralph R. Roberts, of Indiana, was elected Clerk of the House of Representatives of the 86th Congress.

AMENDMENT OF THE RULES

Mr. JOHNSON of Texas. Mr. President, I suggest the absence of a quorum.

THE VICE PRESIDENT. The Secretary will call the roll.

The Chief Clerk proceeded to call the roll.

Mr. JOHNSON of Texas. Mr. President, I ask unanimous consent that the order for the quorum call be rescinded.

THE VICE PRESIDENT. Without objection, it is so ordered.*

Mr. MONRONEY. Mr. President, will the Senator from Texas yield time to me?

Mr. JOHNSON of Texas. I yield to the Senator from Oklahoma.

Mr. MONRONEY. Mr. President, I strongly urge the Members of the Senate to support the motion of the majority leader to proceed to the immediate consideration of the resolution to amend rule XXII.

Mr. JOHNSON of Texas. Mr. President, may we have order?

THE VICE PRESIDENT. The Senate will be in order.

Mr. MONRONEY. Mr. President, I urge such support regardless of any Senator's individual views on the specific amendment of rule XXII which is proposed in the resolution.

If the resolution is made the pending business of the Senate, each Senator will be assured an opportunity to propose whatever alternative he wishes, and to have the Senate express its approval or disapproval of such alternative by majority vote. We are

---

* The device of requesting a quorum call, only to rescind the request, is used to signal absent members that important business is pending on the floor. Quorum bells are rung in all of the offices. Sometimes this device is used specifically to call particular members who are due to speak. See p. 113.

assured, by the adoption of this motion, of an immediate opportunity to vote on a more strict rule of cloture.

This has been the objective which some Members have sought to reach by another means, namely, by a motion that the Senate proceed to adopt rules. . . .

MR. MANSFIELD. I should like to ask the Senator from Oklahoma to yield to me for the purpose of propounding a number of parliamentary inquiries. . . . With the understanding, of course, that the Senator from Oklahoma does not lose the floor.

MR. MONRONEY. I yield with that understanding. . . .

MR. MANSFIELD. My parliamentary inquiry is as follows: I should like to lead up to the inquiry by saying that I am in favor of the Johnson resolution, which I hope will very soon become the pending business. If it does become the pending business, will it be in order to offer a substitute to it in the form of an amendment, to be proposed by the distinguished Senator from Illinois [Mr. Douglas], the distinguished Senator from New York [Mr. Javits], the distinguished Senator from New Jersey [Mr. Case], the distinguished Senator from Minnesota [Mr. Humphrey], and other Senators?

THE VICE PRESIDENT. The resolution will be open to amendment and substitution by any action the Members of the Senate may desire to take in regard to it.

MR. MANSFIELD. I would be opposed to such a substitute proposal. However, if it is offered on that basis, then, under the rules of the Senate, we would vote, first, on the Douglas-Javits-Case-Humphrey proposal. Is that correct?

THE VICE PRESIDENT. If an amendment or substitute is offered, such amendment or substitute would come before the Senate first.

MR. MANSFIELD. Therefore the Senate would have a chance to work its will, on a clear-cut division of votes, first on the bipartisan proposal of the Senators from Illinois, Minnesota, New Jersey, and New York. Is that correct?

THE VICE PRESIDENT. If the Senate so desires, it may so proceed.

MR. MANSFIELD. If Senators desire a yea-and-nay vote, all they have to do is to ask for it, and they will receive it. Is that correct?

THE VICE PRESIDENT. That is correct.

MR. MANSFIELD. Referring to the Anderson resolution, which I am also opposing, could that be offered as a substitute or as an amendment to either the Douglas or Johnson resolution?

THE VICE PRESIDENT. It could be offered as a substitute.

MR. MANSFIELD. On that basis, Mr. President, we could come to a clear-cut vote on that issue, if the Senate so desired.

THE VICE PRESIDENT. That is correct.

MR. MANSFIELD. . . . What I am trying to have made clear is this: There has been talk of hijacking and blackjacking because the majority leader, by reason of his position, was recognized first yesterday and submitted a resolution. As I understand the rulings of the Chair, every Member of the Senate will have a chance to vote yea or nay on the Anderson proposal, on the Douglas proposal, and on the Johnson of Texas proposal. Is not that correct?

THE VICE PRESIDENT. The Senator from Montana is correct. . . .

MR. RUSSELL, MR. JAVITS, and other Senators addressed the Chair.

THE VICE PRESIDENT. Does the Senator from Oklahoma yield; and, if so, to whom?

MR. MONRONEY. I yield first to the Senator from Georgia, under the conditions previously stated.

MR. RUSSELL. Mr. President, I desire to propound a parliamentary inquiry. The Chair has stated on several occasions, and has reiterated this morning, that he is of the opinion that most of the rules of the Senate are applicable here today, and therefore are continuing. There are other rules, to which the Chair referred by rule and by number, as to which the Chair is of the opinion that they are not applicable, for the reason the Chair has stated—namely, that he thinks they are unconstitutional.

I should like to ask the Chair on what rule or what statute or what provision of the Constitution of the United States the Chair, as Presiding Officer of the Senate, relies for this attempt to exercise the right to select which rules of the Senate are applicable and which are not applicable, and which are constitutional and which are unconstitutional.

THE VICE PRESIDENT. The Chair is bound by the rules of the

Senate, as adopted by the Senate. The Chair also has a constitutional responsibility. The Chair has indicated on several occasions, moreover, that while it is the opinion of the Chair that the Senate rules, in the respects to which the Chair has referred, are not in accordance with constitutional mandate, it is only the Chair's opinion, and that question, if it is raised, will be submitted to the Senate itself for its decision.

MR. RUSSELL. Does the Chair arrive at that conclusion of his right to render these advisory opinions under his constitutional position as a member of the executive branch of the Government, or in his status as Presiding Officer of the Senate?

THE VICE PRESIDENT. The Chair renders that opinion in his status as Presiding Officer of the Senate. The Chair should point out he renders this opinion only in response to parliamentary inquiries which have been propounded by various Members of the Senate. . . .

THE VICE PRESIDENT laid before the Senate, Senate Resolution 5, which was read by the legislative clerk, as follows:

> *Resolved,* That subsection 2 of rule XXII of the Standing Rules of the Senate is amended (1) by striking out "except subsection 3 of rule XXII,", and (2) by striking out "two-thirds of the Senators duly chosen and sworn" and inserting in lieu thereof "two-thirds of the Senators present and voting."
>
> SEC. 2. Subsection 3 of rule XXII of the Standing Rules of the Senate is amended by striking out "and of subsection 2 of this rule."
>
> SEC. 3. Rule XXXII of the Standing Rules of the Senate is amended by inserting "1." immediately preceeding "At", and by adding at the end thereof a new paragraph as follows:
>
> "2. The rules of the Senate shall continue from one Congress to the next Congress unless they are changed as provided in these rules."

MR. JOHNSON of Texas. Mr. President, I ask the Senator from Oklahoma if he will permit me to make a brief statement.

MR. MONRONEY. I yield, and ask unanimous consent that I may be permitted to resume my remarks following the statement of the majority leader.

THE VICE PRESIDENT. Is there objection? The Chair hears none and the Senator from Texas may proceed.

MR. JOHNSON of Texas. Mr. President, I should like to say that with respect to the motion proposed by the Senator from New

Mexico [Mr. Anderson] yesterday, or with respect to any motion he may intend to propose today, which involves submitting to the Senate the question of whether it wants to displace the Johnson resolution and go into the question of an entire new set of rules, I will be glad to ask unanimous consent that it be in order to consider that motion today, without having it lie over a day under rule XL; and I make such a request.

THE VICE PRESIDENT. Is there objection? Without objection—— . . .

MR. CASE of New Jersey. Mr. President, reserving the right to object——

MR. DIRKSEN. Mr. President——

MR. MONRONEY. Mr. President, I ask unanimous consent——

THE VICE PRESIDENT. The Senator from Oklahoma has the floor.

MR. MONRONEY. Mr. President, I ask unanimous consent that I may yield to the distinguished minority leader without losing my right to the floor.

MR. ANDERSON. Mr. President, a parliamentary inquiry.

THE VICE PRESIDENT. The Senator will state it.

MR. ANDERSON. Did the Senator from Texas [Mr. Johnson] not propound a unanimous-consent request?

THE VICE PRESIDENT. Does the Senator from Texas desire——

MR. JOHNSON of Texas. . . . I desire to make clear . . . that I do not want to invoke rule XL and further delay this matter. I am willing to have the Senator submit his motion, and then I shall be glad to propound my request. Then the motion can speak for itself.

THE VICE PRESIDENT. Is there objection to the Senator from New Mexico submitting his motion? . . .

MR. ANDERSON. Mr. President, I submit the motion.

THE VICE PRESIDENT. Without objection, the clerk will read the motion.

The Chief Clerk. Mr. Anderson moves "that the Senate, in accordance with article I, section 5 of the Constitution which declares that 'each House may determine the rules of its proceedings' now proceed to the immediate consideration of the adoption of rules for the Senate of the 86th Congress."

THE VICE PRESIDENT. Will the Senator now state his unanimous-consent request? . . .

MR. JOHNSON of Texas. Very well. I ask unanimous consent that, notwithstanding the provisions of rule XL, it may be in order to consider this motion as a substitute for the Johnson resolution. If adopted, of course, it would displace the Johnson resolution and prolong debate even further, in my opinion.

THE VICE PRESIDENT. Is there objection to the unanimous-consent request of the Senator from Texas? Without objection, the unanimous-consent request is agreed to. . . .

MR. JOHNSON of Texas. Mr. President, I should like to notify the attachés on both sides of the aisle and the leadership of the Senate minority that we are hopeful that the Senate may be able to obtain a vote on a motion which I plan to make after Senators who wish to speak on the Anderson motion have done so—namely, a motion to table that motion. I expect to make my motion with the concurrence of the minority leader, at some time agreeable to him, either late this afternoon or perhaps early in the evening, if that course seems to be acceptable to a goodly number of our colleagues. . . .

Mr. President, I shall talk to the various proponents of this measure, because all of us understand that a motion to lay on the table is not debatable. But it should be understood that we do not expect to make such a motion until Members have had an adequate opportunity to express their views. . . .*

[*It took some time, as indicated in the passage just below, for the various parliamentary inquiries and maneuvers to be concluded. Because the procedure followed could mean victory or defeat for the sponsors of the several motions, they felt it essential to fix the ground rules clearly.*]

MR. MONRONEY. . . . Mr. President, . . . the colloquies and parliamentary inquiries which have been going on during the 2 hours I have held the floor have contributed greatly to the educa-

---

* The Majority Leader, in consultation with others of the leadership, fixes the calendar (the schedule of debate) of the Senate. It is customary for him to alert the Senators to the probable schedule of votes, as Mr. Johnson has done here. On this occasion, however, Senator Morse was displeased with the plan, and filibustered to force the vote over to the succeeding day (see pp. 105–106).

tion and enlightenment of the Senate in connection with this complex problem of rules and the adoption of rules. It has been highly instructive to the Senate....

However, it seems to me that the important thing—and it speaks more eloquently than anything I could ever say on the subject—is that the enlightenment of the Senate which has resulted was based on the little black book I hold in my hand. It is called the Senate Manual. It contains the 40 rules which have come down to us after surviving many periods of change. All the answers which have been given are in the rule book. We are able to proceed today to change the rules in an orderly way, as proposed by the Johnson amendment to change rule XXII, only because we have these rules in the first place.

If the Anderson proposal were to supplant the Johnson proposal, we would have no rules under which to proceed. We would proceed de novo. There would be no limitation on debate, and any Senator who had the floor could hold it. I say that because there would be no rules. There would be no rule that a Senator must proceed in order, or that he must refrain from making derogatory references to his colleagues in the Senate. We would be flying blind, without instruments and without any control points to check. Under the Anderson proposal we would throw out the rule book and say that the Senate rules are not continuing....

Mr. President, I yield the floor.

MR. ANDERSON. Mr. President——

THE PRESIDING OFFICER. The Senator from New Mexico. ...

MR. ANDERSON. Mr. President, my interest in the proposal to adopt rules at the beginning of the session is based upon enough experience to know that if we do not act on the rules now, we will never have opportunity to act during this session. We have been discussing this situation through a number of sessions of Congress. ...

[*Senator Anderson proceeded to review previous unsuccessful attempts to amend the Senate Rules.*]

MR. LONG. Mr. President, will the Senator yield?

MR. ANDERSON. I yield to the Senator from Louisiana.

MR. LONG. Reference has been made to the book I hold in my hand. It has been called the rulebook. Of course, it is the "Senate

Manual," which contains the rules of the Senate. It contains some rules written by Thomas Jefferson, in "Jefferson's Manual." We have followed some of the precedents in "Jefferson's Manual." Thomas Jefferson has not been here for 150 years. Do my colleagues wish with regard to Thomas Jefferson and with respect to the rest of the rules to do the same thing that is proposed?

The book also contains the "Declaration of Independence." Do the Senators wish to throw that out, too, now that Thomas Jefferson is gone?

I see in the book also the Constitution, which was written by men who have not been here for a 150 years. Do Senators wish to do away with those portions of the "Manual"?

MR. PASTORE. Mr. President, will the Senator yield so that I may propound a question?

MR. ANDERSON. I yield.

MR. PASTORE. I should like to ask the Senator from Louisiana. For what rules of the Senate did Thomas Jefferson vote?

MR. LONG. I did not hear the question.

MR. PASTORE. For what rules of the Senate did Thomas Jefferson vote, that we are violating now? We are talking about the right of the Senate to make its own rules. If we do not have rules, we can vote for the parliamentary rules which have been prescribed by Thomas Jefferson, or we can adopt "Robert's Rules of Order." That may be so. All I am saying is that fundamentally, under the Constitution, it has been decided that the Senate can make its own rules. But which Senate? The Senate of 1800 or the Senate of 1959? I say that if the Senate of 1959 has the responsibility to do the people's business, it ought to have the responsibility of adopting its own rules.

MR. LONG. That is what we are trying to do. We are attempting to change some of our rules. Our rules include precedents which have been handed down to us. Those precedents oftentimes are binding on the Senate. They have been adopted together with the rules. . . .

MR. ANDERSON. I was just about to quote Thomas Jefferson. He said:

> Can one generation bind another, and all others, in succession forever?

I think not. The Creator has made the earth for the living, not the dead.

In the Senate of the United States, I say to the Senator from Louisiana, we ought to write rules for the living, not the dead. . . .

MR. O'MAHONEY. Mr. President, will the Senator yield?

MR. ANDERSON. I yield.

MR. O'MAHONEY. I have listened to the interrogations and the answers which have been given, and I should like to ask the Senator from New Mexico another question. Will he be so kind as to tell me why the adoption of the Johnson resolution would deprive the Senate of any power to change rules by a majority vote?

MR. ANDERSON. The Johnson resolution contains section 3, which provides a new section 2, and that section 2 will read:

> The rules of the Senate shall continue from one Congress to the next Congress unless they are changed as provided in these rules.

MR. O'MAHONEY. Are not the rules of the Senate as they now exist, with the exception of rule XXII, against which I shall vote, amply sufficient to allow the Senate to change its rules by majority vote at any time?

MR. ANDERSON. No. I think that ruling has been made, round after round, that it requires a sizable vote—no; not a sizable vote, but a majority vote, to get the question before the Senate.

MR. O'MAHONEY. But the Johnson amendment strikes out that provision.

MR. ANDERSON. It would still require a two-thirds vote to impose cloture. . . .

In the succeeding Congress, the one which will begin in 1961, the able Senator from Wisconsin [Mr. Proxmire] might rise and say, "I move that the rules of the Senate be changed in the following particulars." He must be able to enforce cloture to secure consideration of his motion. He must obtain a two-thirds vote of the Senate to reach that point. . . .

MR. O'MAHONEY. The Senator from New Mexico is not answering my simple question. I should like to know how, by the adoption of the Johnson resolution, we shall deny to the Senate the power, by a majority vote, to change its rules whenever it wants to do so.

Mr. ANDERSON. There is nothing said about a majority vote. I have said it takes a two-thirds vote to get the question up. We could change that if a resolution to change the rules were acted upon, but we could not get such a resolution before the Senate.

Mr. O'MAHONEY. No one is objecting to bringing up the Johnson resolution except the Senator from New Mexico and his associates.

Mr. ANDERSON. The Senator from Wyoming should not say that. . . .

Mr. MORSE. The Senator will recall that we could not get to a vote in 1949 until the southern bloc released the Senate so that it could vote, after the signing of the round robin which pledged Senators in advance, guaranteeing that the so-called Wherry resolution would be adopted; is that not the case?

Mr. ANDERSON. That is absolutely the case.

Mr. MORSE. I want to stress it.

Mr. ANDERSON. We could not get to any kind of a vote. Hour after hour new records were being set. Some of us took courses on how to fulibuster. One Senator said, "Tilt back and forth." It was said one should not take liquids for 24 hours before starting. We were told to teeter back and forth on our feet, so that the muscles would not get sore. Some others had different divices. We had a whole course on filibustering given to us in the U.S. Senate. . . .

But the important thing is that nobody in the U.S. Senate could vote on one important thing. No committee could meet. . . .

The night of the round robin was a night long to remember. It was a night we were told, "You will never have a chance to vote on anything until, on your hands and knees, you agree this sort of thing will be done."

Round robins were circulated by which Senators pledged themselves to vote for this one thing and this one thing only, and nothing else would come to the floor of the Senate until that was done. The Senate was tied up for weeks, and could not do a thing until that action was taken. I believed then, and I believe now, that that sort of force should be blocked. I believed then, and I believe now, that the only way to do this is by the motion I have put forward. If I thought there were an easy or simple way to do it, I would have done it long ago, because this has been on my heart steadily from that day on. . . .

Mr. HUMPHREY and Mr. CLARK addressed the Chair.

Mr. ANDERSON. If the Senator from Pennsylvania does not mind, I should like to yield to the Senator from Minnesota. I mentioned the Senator a minute ago.

Mr. HUMPHREY. . . . One of the strange paradoxes of the situation relating to the Senate rules is the fact that the Senator from New Mexico is standing on the floor today defending the great constitutional principle, the Federal principle, the principle of States rights; and some of the advocates of States rights are attempting to destroy it. Let me explain what I mean.

The so-called Connecticut compromise on the Constitution, relating to the large States and the small States involved in the constitutional convention, provided that, regardless of the size of the State or the population of the State, each State should have two Senators, and each Senator should have equal voting rights and equal privileges. Senators who are trying to deny to the U.S. Senate the privilege of exercising its constitutional right of adopting rules are doing so in violation of a fundamental principle of the American Constitution.

I ask my colleagues to bear with me on this point. What right is there on the part of any group in the Senate to deny to 18 newly elected U.S. Senators the opportunity to have something to say about the rules under which they are to participate in the deliberations of this body? . . .

Mr. RUSSELL. . . . Any rule that gags the representatives of sovereign States from exercising their right to speak in the forum of States does not meet with my approval. . . .

Mr. DOUGLAS. . . . I shall try to speak briefly, but I shall try to make clear why we believed the Anderson motion is essential. . . .

Underneath all the verbiage, underneath all the parliamentary maneuvers, . . . We are trying to establish at the very beginning of the Senate the right of the Senate, by a majority vote, to adopt rules, and not to be governed by the straitjacket which was imposed in 1949. . . .

I am astounded by the contention that the Senate, which is declared to be such a deliberative body, composed of such noble and reasonable men, who have a high sense of the values of the Nation, will simply prove itself inferior to the House of Representatives, which deals with this issue very quickly—very quickly indeed—at the opening of a new Congress. I do not claim that we are the higher body. . . . I do not say that everything the House can do, the Senate can do better; but I do say everything the House can do, the Senate can do as well. . . .

I regret that my good friend from Georgia used the expression this afternoon that the Senate consisted of ambassadors from their sovereign States. That, perhaps, was the interpretation, under the Articles of Confederation, and the Delegates to the Continental Congress I think, perhaps, primarily regarded themselves as such.

But we are a United States now—and have been a United States for at least 93 years. I regret to see the pre-1860 language used upon the floor of the Senate at the present time. We are not merely Senators from Minnesota, Pennsylvania, Illinois, Alaska, Ohio, Michigan, Utah, North Carolina, Florida, Louisiana, Georgia, Alabama, and South Carolina; we are also Senators of the United States of America. It is about time that fact is realized. . . .

I am not here to wave the bloody shirt. . . . I will merely say that since 1865, at least, the United States is a nation . . . and we meet in one House of that Nation, representing our State interests, it is true, but also representing our national interests, and the national interests should be controlling and predominant.

What bearing does that have on this dispute? It has this bearing: that the Senate is not an assembly of the United Nations. Neither is it a Security Council of the United Nations. No one in this body should have the power of the veto. No small groups should have the power of the veto.

The Constitution provides that the majority will is to prevail except in those matters which are specifically stated to the contrary, and there are only five such. The Constitution states that amendments to the Constitution must be submitted by a two-thirds vote of both Houses; that treaties must be ratified by a two-thirds vote of the Senate; that impeachment requires a two-thirds vote; that expulsion of a Member requires a two-thirds vote; and that to override a veto a two-thirds vote is required.

But on every other subject a majority is supposed to prevail, in default of specific language to the contrary. There is no such language about House rules or Senate rules. There is no such provision in the Constitution in connection with civil rights laws. . . .

It is therefore perfectly clear where the Constitution stands. The Constitution stands for majority rule, but a majority rule which is carefully guarded—which requires the assent of both Houses, which is subject to a Presidential veto and subject to review by the courts.

We already have built-in protections for minorities and other groups, and long may we continue to have them.

Furthermore, by the so-called Connecticut compromise . . . we have equality of representation in the Senate of all States regardless of size. . . .

As a matter of fact, 17 States with only 8 percent of the population could, if acting in a bloc, under the existing rules of the Senate and under the rules as proposed by the Senator from Texas, by filibustering, tie up the Senate and prevent the representatives of the other 92 percent of the population from having their will. . . .

What I am trying to say is that we already have built-in protections for minorities even under a majority provision; protection in the form of two Houses of Congress, protection in the form of the presidential veto; protection in the form of judicial review; and protection to the small States on the basis of equality of representation.

If on top of all this we have heaped upon us the power of a small group in the Senate to prevent us even from coming to a vote, there will be placed mighty and powerful chains upon us. . . .

We believe in full debate, full discussion—protracted debate, because many issues need to be made clear, not merely to the Senate, but to the country. But we believe that there is also the right of a majority at some time to reach a vote. The right of the majority to rule does not mean merely that when the ballot is cast the majority shall prevail. The right of the majority also to have a measure ultimately brought up for a vote is also an essential part of the right of majority rule. That is what we are contending for . . . .

[*The debate was not without its lighter moments:*]

MR. HUMPHREY. Mr. President, will the Senator yield further?
MR. DOUGLAS. I am glad to yield.
MR. HUMPHREY. So that we may have this matter in the simple

and direct language and tie down the principal points and the argument being made by the proponents of the Anderson motion, there are those who have attempted to confuse the American people and even Members of the Senate. I do not say that the attempt has been made with premeditation, but, rather, because of misunderstanding. The attempt has been made to confuse people on the subject of the Senate being a continuing body, when in fact, as has been pointed out repeatedly in the debate, that phrase, which has been applied to the Senate, applies to the two-thirds membership of the Senate, not to its legislative responsibility.

MR. DOUGLAS. That contention, as W. S. Gilbert has mentioned in the "Mikado," like the flowers that bloom in the spring, tra la, has nothing to do with the case. The question is whether the existing Senate shall be bound by rules, adopted long ago, which operate in many cases to prevent a vote on a proposal which the majority of the Senate wishes to adopt. . . .

MR. CLARK. Mr. President, will the Senator yield?

MR. DOUGLAS. I yield.

MR. CLARK. A minute or two ago the distinguished Senator from Illinois had occasion to comment on the continuing body theory in terms of Gilbert and Sullivan's "Mikado." I should like to recall to my good friend some lines from the "Mikado" which immediately follow the lines he has quoted and which I believe are equally pertinent to the continuing body theory. As I recall those lines from my youth, they run something like this:

> I've got to take under my wing,
>   Tra la.
> A most unattractive old thing,
>   Tra la.

MR. DOUGLAS. "With a caricature of a face."

MR. CLARK. With a caricature of a face. . . .

MR. THURMOND. Mr. President, I cannot help but feel that the Senate itself, as an institution, is at this moment under attack and in peril of destruction. As is so often the case, the most imminent danger to this, as to many other institutions, lies from within rather than from without. Surely the proponents of the pending motion do not envisage the depth and breadth of their proposal.

Tradition, in and of itself, is no complete answer to any problem. Nevertheless, longstanding traditions are seldom maintained without sufficient reason. Almost invariably, traditions serve as a warning beacon of obscure, but sound and logical, purposes. . . .

The Senate is not an ordinary parliamentary body. Analogies to the procedure of other parliamentary bodies have little, if any, relevancy to the question before us. For instance, the House of Representatives is exclusively a legislative body. The Senate is far more. In addition to being a legislative body, it performs, by constitutional mandate, both executive and judicial functions. Article II, section 2 of the Constitution provides that the President shall share with the Senate his executive treaty-making power and his power of appointment of the officers of the United States. Article I, section 3 of the Constitution requires of the Senate a judicial function by reposing in the Senate the sole power to try all impeachments.

The uniqueness of the Senate is not confined, by any means, to its variety of functions. There are innumerable other aspects about this body which prevent its orderly operation at any time under parliamentary law other than its own rules, adopted in accordance with the provisions of those rules. For example, almost all parliamentary procedures presuppose that any main question, after due notice, can be decided by at least a majority of the members of the particular body using the parliamentary procedure. Any Senate rules which presupposed such a conclusion would be inoperable, for the Constitution itself specifies the necessity for two-thirds majority for action on many matters.

. . . The very fact that each State, regardless of its population, has equal representation in this body belies the thought of simple majority rule in its deliberation.

It is this very uniqueness which has compelled so many to conclude that the Senate had a degree of continuity unknown to other parliamentary bodies.

The Founding Fathers themselves, in drafting the Constitution, provided for this continuity by establishing a 6-year term of office for each Senator, so that a minimum of two-thirds of the entire body would continue from one session to the next. Had the Founding Fathers desired continuity only, but less than a continuing body, they could have provided for a staggered term of 4 years for a Senator with one-half of the Senate returning from one session to the next. This would not have provided the necessary quorums to do business at all times, and the Senate would not have been a continuing body.

The Senate itself has reenforced the premise that it is a continuing body by the unbroken precedent of continuing its rule from one session to the next. . . .

MR. CASE of New Jersey. Mr. President, I rise in support of the motion of the Senator from New Mexico [Mr. Anderson]. . . .

Mr. President, to me the issue seems simple and clear. It is, no more or no less, whether the Members of the Senate shall be allowed to review the rules under which they must operate.

I realize that, as in the past, those opposing amendment of the Senate rules argue that, unlike the House, the Senate is a continuing body, and that therefore its rules continue, without readoption, from one Congress to the next. . . . But even more convincing arguments can be made to the contrary.

In every major activity the Senate recognizes a constitutional right of the Senate of each new Congress to determine anew both legislative and executive business. All consideration of bills, resolutions, treaties, and nominations starts at the beginning of each Congress without reference to, or continuation of, what has taken place in the past; new officers and committee members are elected in the Senate of each new Congress; when the Senate finally adjourns, the slate is wiped clean; the proceedings begin again in the next Congress.

Indeed, the thing that stands out in any thorough analysis is that—apart from membership—everything starts afresh. And rules, too, start afresh the moment a majority of the Senators at the opening of the Senate of a new Congress so will it and so vote. . . .

MR. TALMADGE. Mr. President——

THE PRESIDING OFFICER. The Senator from Georgia.

MR. TALMADGE. Mr. President, the proposal that the Senate adopt new rules involves considerably more than a mere question of the procedure to be followed in this Chamber.

Its ramifications extend to the very heart of our form of government and candor compels the conclusion that the effect of its approval would be to repudiate the Senate's assigned constitutional role.

It is vital, therefore, Mr. President, that this question be resolved not from the standpoint of any transient advantage which might accrue to some partisan group but rather on the basis of its implications for the future of constitutional, republican government in this Nation.

The United States Senate, in the light of history and the Constitution, is much more than another legislative body.

It is, in reality, a continuing council of States sitting as an integral part of the Federal establishment—a protective repository on the national level for the sovereignty of the sovereign States.

It was with plain design that our Founding Fathers created it as a watchman over all operations of our National Government.

And it was with deliberate intent that they conferred upon it the broadest powers to act as a checkmate on unwarranted centralization of authority.

Our far-seeing forefathers well realized that the House of Representatives would be both too large and too impermanent to fulfill those desired objectives.

They knew there could never be free debate in the House and that important bills would pass that chamber without sufficient study and deliberation.

And, perceiving those problems, they put their faith in the United States Senate and bestowed upon it the major responsibility for keeping faith with posterity. . . .

All of the great injustices of history have been committed in the name of unchecked and unbridled majority rule.

The late Senator James A. Reed, of Missouri, in one of the most forceful speeches ever delivered before the Senate, observed with great truth that:

> The majority crucified Jesus Christ.
> The majority burned the Christians at the stake.
> The majority drove the Jews into exile and to ghetto.
> The majority established slavery.
> The majority chained to stakes and surrounded with circles of flame martyrs through all the ages of the world's history.

The majority jeered when Columbus said the world was round.
The majority threw him into a dungeon for having discovered a new world.
The majority said that Galileo must recant or that Galileo must go to prison.
The majority cut off the ears of John Pym because he dared advocate the liberty of the press. . . .

It is essential to our interests as a Nation that we keep vital and inviolate our system of checks and balances of which the continuing nature of the Senate and freedom of debate within it are integral parts.

With continuity of direction and unlimited debate in the United States Senate, all Americans have the assurance that no act jeopardizing their rights ever will be proposed without some Member of the Senate having the opportunity to resist it and to warn the Nation of its consequences. . . .

MR. SPARKMAN. . . . The upper House of the National Legislature is not just another assembly of lawmakers. It is a very special organization and this must be kept in mind whenever the expediencies of the moment seem to necessitate some changes in its mode of operating,

The kind of body that the Senate is will readily be understood on examination of the basis upon which the Republic was founded and the Constitution adopted. In order to induce the several States to cede a portion of their sovereignty to the National Government, it was necessary to insure to the States that the portion of sovereignty not given up would be protected, and that all States, regardless of their size and population, would have an equal voice in the Senate. In order to accomplish these purposes, the Senate was created, composed of two Members from each State, at first chosen by the State legislatures. The Senate was originally envisioned as an assemblage of ambassadors from the States, in part at least, wherein could be heard the voices of those representing the States as States.

The Members of the House of Representatives speak as representatives of special districts within their States and for the interests of their own particular localities. But when a United States Senator stands up to speak in the Senate, he speaks not for an arbitrarily marked-off district within his State, but for the whole State and all its people. Whenever he addresses the Senate, one is necessarily reminded of that special relationship existing between the Federal Government and the States, created by the Constitution when it bestowed certain enumerated powers upon the National Government and reserved the rest to the States....

The Senate is the embodiment and preserver of this relationship between the State government and the National Government. Diminish it to the level of the ordinary body of elected representatives and the federation of States which makes up the Union will turn into another power state, with a strong and dominant central government and 49 provinces....

Inherent in the idea of popular representative government is the belief that the elected representatives of the people should remain responsive to the well-informed and enlightened will of the people. It is becoming increasingly difficult to keep the representatives of the people in real touch with those who chose them, but to a very real extent this is done in the case of the Senate. In that body, both by tradition and according to the fundamental concepts of the Constitution, a great measure of free debate and deliberation exists. This enables the Members of the Senate to slow down the impetus given to proposed legislation by the headlong procedures of the House, and hold new measures, so to speak, up before the public gaze.

The Senate sits in a sort of appellate capacity with respect to proposed laws. It is its duty to go carefully over them, and this can hardly be done without ample freedom of debate....

Another important aspect of the Senate's function is its force as a check upon the executive branch of the Government. For this purpose it is imperative that the Senate be permitted complete freedom to express itself; otherwise, it would fall submissive on many occasions to presidential and party autocracy, thus vitiating the idea of the separation of powers so essential to our system of Government....

Mr. Sparkman. Mr. President, I yield the floor.

Mr. Morse. Mr. President, at the beginning of this speech I wish to call attention to rule XIX, and then I wish to propound a parliamentary inquiry.

Paragraph 1 of rule XIX reads as follows:

1. When a Senator desires to speak, he shall rise and address the Presiding Officer, and shall not proceed until he is recognized, and the Presiding Officer shall recognize the Senator who shall first address him. No Senator shall interrupt another Senator in debate without his consent, and to obtain such consent, he shall first address the Presiding Officer, and no Senator shall speak more than twice upon any one question in debate on the same day without leave of the Senate, which shall be determined without debate.

My parliamentary inquiry is as follows: Am I correct in my assumption that this is my first speech on the issue now before the Senate, under rule XIX?

THE PRESIDING OFFICER (Mr. McGee in the chair). The pending question is the proposal of the Senator from New Mexico; and this is the first speech of the Senator from Oregon on that proposal.

MR. MORSE. Mr. President, I ask for the ruling because in the very introduction of this speech I wish to make clear the purposes of the speech; and it has more than one purpose. . . .

Mr. President, on yesterday I sought to participate in discussing this overall issue. I was on my feet several times for that purpose. In fact, I was on my feet, seeking the floor in my own right, when the majority leader moved that the Senate adjourn. . . .

Now, there is no question about the parliamentary right of the majority leader to make his motion to adjourn. But making the motion to adjourn did not, Mr. President, protect what I always thought was the proposal of those holding to the point of view of the majority leader on the merits of the general legislative issue before the Senate—that they believed in full debate in the Senate. . . . What is involved in effect, Mr. President, was an imposition of cloture upon Members of the Senate who wanted to proceed yesterday to discuss the issue on its merits. . . .

The procedure followed today, Mr. President, was also procedure that I do not intend to support, so long as I am in the Senate. . . .

Mr. President, for decades liberals in the Senate of the United States have had to protect their minority rights by exercising their rights under the rules of the Senate. I remember that after the first speech I made in the Senate in 1945, young Bob LaFollette, a distinguished Senator from Wisconsin at that time, came over and sat down along side of me after I had finished. He said to me, "I have a bit of advice to give to you. Make a study of the rules of the Senate and, as a liberal, be ready to exercise your prerogatives under those rules, when movements are on in the Senate to use the rules for the purpose of steamrolling tactics or to defeat the type of legislation that the public interest calls for, and for which liberals are renowned to stand."

I have followed that advice through 14 years in the Senate, and I am following it tonight. . . .

Mr. President, . . . I am one liberal who admits that he filibusters. I am the only one I know of in the Senate who has ever stood on the floor of the Senate and said, "I am participating in a filibuster."

I suppose in a certain sense this is a filibuster tonight. I said in the beginning that one of the purposes of my speech is to stop a vote on the Anderson motion tonight. I expect to be successful in that objective, at least on the basis of my present good feeling. . . .

I have filibustered, and will again, for the length of time necessary to make certain that we have laid before the Senate the evidence on the merits of a legislative issue, and which we believe the Senate and the country ought to consider before a final vote is taken on the issue. . . .

[*The Senator's "good feeling" stood him in good stead. His speech, inclusive of insertions in the* Record *which were not actually read on the floor, occupied approximately thirty-three pages. The closing passages which follow show how the victory of the filibuster was signalled.*]

Mr. President, while waiting for word from a staff member as to the pleasure of the leadership of the Senate as to whether I shall make a motion for the Senate to take a recess, I do not need to read what I was going to read. Instead, I am having printed in the *Record* the position of the Democratic President of 1949 on cloture.

Mr. President, I have closed this first speech, and obviously the only speech I shall have to make before the vote is taken, on tomorrow, on the Anderson motion.

. . . Mr. President, in accordance with the previous order, I now move that the Senate stand in recess until tomorrow morning, at 10 o'clock.

Friday, January 9, 1959

MR. MANSFIELD. Mr. President, the present discussion is one which offers great scope for the talents of lawyers and parliamentarians. As the Senate knows, we have in our midst many brilliant lawyers. We have among us many outstanding parliamentarians.

We have already heard from several of these able Members. Before we are done with this debate, I am sure that we shall have heard from them all. They will marshal the relevant precedents. Through them, great voices of the past which once thundered on the same issues may be expected to speak to us again. Some shall be made to speak on one side of the issues. Others on the other side. And still others on both sides. We shall hear not only from the able Senators from the North and the able Senators from the South who are with us today; we shall hear also from the able Senators of another era, from North, South, East and West. . . .

The experience of being led into the great treasure house of legal and parliamentary wisdom is indeed exhilarating and exalting. But, I regret to say, it is also exhausting. . . .

. . . We find ourselves informed of all the legal, historic, and parliamentary reasons for doing or not doing some particular thing. The only trouble is that, by that time, we have forgotten what it was we had set out to do. . . .

Mr. President, unless my perception deceives me, what is basically at issue in this discussion is not the continuity of the Senate. The issue is not civil rights. It is not even the majority will and how it is to be expressed in voting. The basic issue is far more profound and at the same time far more simple than is indicated by the debate which has so far taken place. What we are really concerned with is the place of the Senate in the pattern of political institutions which holds together this vast, complex, living and changing Nation. We shall not get on the main path of that issue, however, if we run down the sidepaths, deeper and deeper into the thickets of continuing body, civil rights, and majority rule.

. . . Mr. President, the Senate is here, regardless of whether eminent gentlemen of the past or present say it is not supposed to be.

. . . The Founding Fathers would have been the first to guide, but they would have been the last to try to control us. The job of understanding the role of the Senate today is our job, not theirs. . . . One part of this role has been touched upon many times, in discussions and commentary on the nature of the Senate. We are, it is said, the long-termers; and we are the few. Some writers even go so far as to call us the solons. These characteristics presumably permit us to remain unmoved by the sudden tidal waves which from time to time descend upon the political life of popular government. . . .

Assuming that we do have the function of standing against the tidal waves, does it follow that, in the exercise of this function, the Senate may block the long tides of our history? That is not the exercise of the function: that is an abuse of the function. . . .

If one function of the Senate, then, is to stand against the tidal waves without blocking the tides, another is to facilitate, to regulate the adjustment of all sections of the Nation to these tides. . . .

There are strong bonds which unite all Americans, regardless of where they may live. But, let us face it: There are also sectional differences in predominant mores and customs, in predominant interests, hopes, and fears. This body, perhaps, more than any other in the Federal system should serve—indeed, it must serve—to prevent these differences from widening into unbridgeable gulfs. . . .

To discharge these unique functions, a primary tool of the Senate is the rule of full discussion. The tool is needed to inform; it is needed to prevent unthinking action. . . .

THE VICE PRESIDENT. . . . Under the order previously entered, the Senator from Texas [Mr. Johnson] is recognized.

MR. JOHNSON of Texas. Mr. President, I move to lay on the table the modified amendment of the Senator from New Mexico [Mr. Anderson], in the nature of a substitute for Senate Resolution 5. . . .

THE VICE PRESIDENT. . . . The motion is not debatable. The clerk will call the roll. . . .

The result was announced—yeas 60, nays 36. . . .

MR. JOHNSON of Texas. Mr. President, . . . We expect to ask the Senate to stay in session late this evening, in the hope that a vote can be reached on some of the amendments to rule XXII. If all Senators who wish to offer amendments to rule XXII will

THE DEBATE ON THE SENATE RULES CHANGE, 1959

return to the Chamber, we shall consider whatever amendments may be called up and try to dispose of them as early as possible.

BIRTHDAY ANNIVERSARY OF THE VICE PRESIDENT

MR. DIRKSEN. Mr. President, there is one civil right which cannot be alien to anyone, and that is the celebration of a man's birthday. Today is the 46th anniversary of the birth of the Vice President of the United States. [Applause, Senators rising.] ...

[*Because there is no effective rule of germaneness in the Senate, little interruptions of this sort are not uncommon. There is a ritual about a birthday, however, which is shown in the extracts which follow.*]

MR. JOHNSON of Texas. Mr. President, I join with the distinguished minority leader in wishing the Vice President a very happy birthday. ...

MR. KUCHEL. Mr. President, on behalf of my colleague, the distinguished junior Senator from California [Mr. Engle], and myself, let the record clearly show that the people of California, and the country, wholeheartedly salute the Vice President of the United States, a distinguished son of the State of California, on the occasion of the anniversary of his birthday. ...

MR. SALTONSTALL. Mr. President, I simply wish to add to what the Senator from California has said that his remarks extend beyond the limits of California and include the best wishes of the people of the entire country.

MR. GOLDWATER. Mr. President, I would not want the opportunity to pass without calling attention to the fact that the distinguished Vice President spent several years of his life in Arizona and has been made the healthy, intelligent man he is by Arizona's water. [Laughter.]

AMENDMENT OF THE RULES

The Senate resumed the consideration of the resolution (S. Res. 5) proposing to amend Senate rules XXII and XXXII. ...

[*The pleasant interlude over, the Senate showed another side to its nature:*]

MR. JOHNSON of Texas. Mr. President, will the Chair state the pending business?

THE PRESIDING OFFICER. The Chair lays before the Senate the unfinished business, Senate Resolution 5. . . .

MR. JOHNSON of Texas. Mr. President, I am prepared to vote on Senate Resolution 5. In the Senate we have discussed a proposed rule change every year for several years. It has been 10 years since rule XXII was revised.

I am informed some of my colleagues desire to deliberate in private before concluding just what course will be followed in connection with certain amendments. I am also informed many Senators would like to be free this evening to attend certain meetings they have arranged. But I am hopeful the Senate can proceed with dispatch on this very important matter and try to resolve it. . . .

I am prepared to enter into a unanimous-consent agreement on the majority vote proposal, the substitute which would provide for a majority vote, if that is agreeable to the proponents. . . .

MR. DOUGLAS. Mr. President, will the majority leader yield to me?

MR. JOHNSON of Texas. I yield.

MR. DOUGLAS. Is it the intention of the majority leader to make an affirmative argument for Senate Resolution 5, or is he going to press for a vote without any affirmative argument on Senate Resolution 5?

MR. JOHNSON of Texas. The Senator from Texas . . . reserves the right to control his own speech in such a manner as he may determine to be in the best interests of the country and of the Senate.

MR. DOUGLAS. I know the Senator from Texas will do that, but I also observe he is pushing for a very quick vote. I think . . . we would normally expect that those presenting the resolution would argue in some detail the alleged merits of the proposal which the Senator from Texas is advancing.

MR. JOHNSON of Texas. And if they did argue it in very much detail it would be criticized as being a southern filibuster.

MR. DOUGLAS. No; not at all.

MR. JOHNSON of Texas. I suggest that the Senator from Illinois attempt to guide himself and control his own conduct without attempting to direct the activities of his colleagues.

MR. DOUGLAS. I was not trying to guide the activities of the Senator from Texas in the slightest. In the first place, I would have no desire to do so. In the second place, I know I would be completely ineffective if I did offer such suggestions.

I thought possibly the Senator from Texas, feeling his high obligation to the tradition of the Senate, would not try to railroad his proposal through——

Mr. Johnson of Texas. Oh, the Senator——

Mr. Douglas. Just a moment, please—without an adequate explanation as to what it is he is proposing.

Mr. Johnson of Texas. First, I will say to the Senator that I do not know how long it takes to explain a thing to him. . . .

Mr. President, I am prepared to make a unanimous-consent request for next week, if that is satisfactory to the Senate. I should like to see if the minority would be willing to agree to have a session on Saturday, and a session on Monday, and proceed to vote on amendments after the morning hour on Monday, with 2 hours allotted to each amendment. I make such a unanimous consent request.

The Presiding Officer. Is there objection?

Mr. Douglas. Mr. President, reserving the right to object, I wonder if the eminent and distinguished Senator from Texas would be willing to clarify his request a bit. Is he proposing that there be 2 hours on Monday on each amendment?

Mr. Johnson of Texas. Yes.

Mr. Douglas. And how much time on final passage?

Mr. Johnson of Texas. Whatever is desirable—perhaps an hour to a side. Senators have heard these questions thoroughly discussed.

Mr. Douglas. I wonder if the Senator from Texas would be willing to write out his proposal, so that we may see whether or not there is any fine print in it, and be able to study it in some detail.

Mr. Johnson of Texas. I shall be glad to do that, if the Senator can see better than he can hear. [Laughter.]

Mr. Douglas. I think it is always important to study the fine print in a document submitted by the Senator from Texas.

Mr. Johnson of Texas. . . . I reiterate my request. I ask the Parliamentarian to write it down, or type it, if necessary, and present it to the Senator from Illinois. I ask the Parliamentarian to be sure that it is written in the largest print available, because the Senator from Illinois has difficulty in seeing the fine print. . . .

Mr. Humphrey. Mr. President, will the Senator yield?

Mr. Johnson of Texas. I yield.

Mr. Humphrey. I am sure the Senator will have no difficulty with his unanimous-consent agreement; but he must be a little tolerant in this connection.

Mr. Johnson of Texas. The Senator from Texas is always tolerant.

Mr. Humphrey. The Senator is always tolerant.

Mr. Johnson of Texas. I thank the Senator. . . .

Mr. Johnson of Texas. Mr. President, on behalf of the distinguished minority leader and myself, I submit a proposed unanimous-consent agreement.

The Presiding Officer. The agreement will be read:

The legislative clerk read, as follows:

Ordered, That, effective on Monday, January 12, 1959, at the conclusion of routine morning business, during the further consideration of the resolution (S. Res. 5) to amend rules XXII and XXXII of the Standing Rules of the Senate, debate on any amendment, or amendments to amendments, motion, or appeal, except a motion to lay on the table, shall be limited to 2 hours, to be equally divided and controlled by the mover of any such amendment or motion and the majority leader: *Provided,* That in the event the majority leader is in favor of any such amendment or motion, the time in opposition thereto shall be controlled by the minority leader or some Senator designated by him: *Provided further,* That no amendment that is not germane to the provisions of the said resolution shall be received.

Ordered further, That on the question of the final passage of the said resolution debate shall be limited to 4 hours, to be equally divided and controlled, respectively, by the majority and minority leaders: *Provided,* That the said leaders or either of them, may, from the time under their control on the passage of said resolution, yield additional time to any Senator during the consideration of any amendment, motion, or appeal. . . .

The Presiding Officer. Is there objection to the unanimous-consent request? The Chair hears none, and it is entered.

Monday, January 12, 1959

The Senate resumed the consideration of the resolution (S. Res. 5) proposing to amend Senate rules XXII and XXXII.

The Presiding Officer. The question is on agreeing to the amendment offered by the Senator from Illinois [Mr. Douglas], for himself and other Senators, providing for a majority vote on cloture after 15 days of debate.

MR. STENNIS. Mr. President, . . . As a practical matter, in the passage of highly important legislation in the economic field, as well as in other fields of activity, the present rules of the Senate are the most powerful ally of a Member of the Senate or a small group of Members of the Senate, whether they have been in the Senate only a day, or a week, or a month, or a year, or 20 years.

There have been notable illustrations of that fact, for instance, in the case of the Colorado River project, wherein, through debate, and through a spirit of compromise and some outright delay, a sounder bill for all of the States involved came forth. . . .

Another example is the cotton acreage bill, a highly important measure to many cotton producers. A more just distribution of acreage was forced through the Senate by virtue of a liberal rule on debate. . . .

THE PRESIDING OFFICER (Mr. Morton in the chair). Does the Senator from Illinois desire to yield time?

MR. DOUGLAS. Mr. President, I suggest the absence of a quorum.

MR. JOHNSON of Texas. Mr. President——

THE PRESIDING OFFICER. The time necessary for the calling of the roll will be taken out of the time of the Senator from Illinois. Does the Senator from Illinois understand the time necessary will be taken from his time?

MR. DOUGLAS. Mr. President, there are several Senators on our side of the aisle who wish to speak on the proposal who are not present in the Chamber, or whose remarks have not been prepared. I should be very glad to yield some time to our good friends of the other side of the aisle.

MR. JAVITS. Mr. President, if the Senator from Illinois will yield, we are in much the same situation. . . .

MR. DOUGLAS. Mr. President, I ask unanimous consent that the time necessary for the calling of the roll not be taken from our time. . . .

[*The Majority Leader objected, thus refusing unanimous consent, but ultimately he allowed the time for the quorum call to be charged equally to both sides. With the absent senators thus recalled to duty, the debate continued.*]

Mr. McNamara. Mr. President, there is no doubt that the Senate currently is engaged in one of its most historic debates.

Years from now parliamentarians and students of government will look back on these pages of the *Congressional Record* to study the words we are speaking here. . . .

Mr. Case of New Jersey. Mr. President, for the last few weeks there has been a widespread attempt to make it appear that the proposal offered by the distinguished majority leader offers a reasonable position midway between two extremes.

This is simply not so. . . .

We are told that our proposed new rule might result in a profound change in what for nearly two centuries has been our most changeless institution, the United States Senate, and would end the Senate as a unique deliberative body.

We are accused of regarding conduct described as respect for constitutional tradition as reactionary hostility to civil rights.

Yet the same writer has elsewhere characterized the Senate as "to a most peculiar degree, a southern institution—the South's unending revenge upon the North for Gettysburg."

No, Mr. President; the Senate has not been our most nearly changeless institution. Constitutional tradition, such as there is of it, bearing on the rules issue, is on our side, and not on the side of reactionary hostility to civil rights.

The Senate has undergone radical changes from time to time, and the stultifying veto by filibuster is a comparatively modern curse unknown to the early Senate. . . .

Mr. Javits. . . . Mr. President, what those who oppose this plan are really contending for is the proposition that the power represented in the Senate by two Senators from each State is the power of the State rather than the power of the Senate. . . .

The whole concept of the argument against the proposal before us in the amendment is that the sovereignty of the States is what is represented by the Senators in this body. Obviously, this is completely contrary to the Constitution of the United States, which specifically said that this is not a chamber of States; it is a Chamber of Senators. If we have any doubt about that, the adoption of the amendment for the popular election of Senators certainly put an end to doubt on that question. . . .

Mr. Humphrey. Mr. President, it is quite obvious that the

purpose of these remarks is to state for the *Record* the conviction and opinions and facts which motivate some of us. . . .

[*The debate "for the record" went on, nevertheless. Amendments were disposed of, and the debate on the main motion (the Johnson Resolution) finally concluded as follows:*]

MR. JOHNSON of Texas. Mr. President, are there any other requests for time?

Several Senators. Vote! Vote! Vote!

MR. JOHNSON of Texas. Does the minority leader have any requests for time?

Mr. President, I want to make a brief statement and then I shall suggest the absence of a quorum. If the aids of the Senators will notify Senators, we will proceed to a final vote on the resolution.

Mr. President, I ask for the yeas and nays on the resolution.

THE PRESIDING OFFICER. The yeas and nays have been requested. Is there a sufficient second?

The yeas and nays were ordered.

MR. JOHNSON of Texas. Mr. President, many have said—many times for many purposes—that the Senate could not and would never change rule XXII. . . .

Yet, here we are, ready to bring the changing of rule XXII to a decision on this, our third full working day of the session.

I think the Senate deserves commendation and respect for proceeding as it has. I also believe that some would do well to reexamine their appraisals of the will of the American people. . . .

Mr. President, I yield back the remainder of my time on condition that the minority leader will do likewise.

MR. DIRKSEN. Mr. President, I yield back the remainder of my time.

MR. JOHNSON of Texas. I suggest the absence of a quorum.

THE PRESIDING OFFICER. All time having expired or been yielded back, the Secretary will call the roll.

The legislative clerk proceeded to call the roll.

MR. JOHNSON of Texas. Mr. President, I ask unanimous consent that the order for the quorum call be rescinded.

THE PRESIDING OFFICER. Without objection, it is so ordered. . . . The yeas and nays have been ordered.

The question is on agreeing to the resolution of the Senator from Texas [Mr. Johnson]. The yeas and nays have been ordered, and the clerk will call the roll.

The legislative clerk proceeded to call the roll.

MR. YOUNG of North Dakota (when his name was called). On this vote I have a pair with the senior Senator from New Hampshire [Mr. Bridges]. If he were present and voting, he would vote "yea"; if I were permitted to vote, I would vote "nay." I therefore withhold my vote.

The rollcall was concluded.

MR. MANSFIELD. I announce that the Senator from Oregon [Mr. Neuberger] is absent because of illness.

I further announce that, if present and voting the Senator from Oregon [Mr. Neuberger], would vote "yea."

MR. DIRKSEN. I announce that the Senator from New Hampshire [Mr. Bridges] is absent on official business and his pair has been previously announced by the Senator from North Dakota [Mr. Young].

The Senator from South Dakota [Mr. Mundt] is absent on official business and if present and voting, he would vote "yea."

The result was announced—yeas 72, nays 22, as follows:

YEAS—72

Aiken	Chavez	Hartke
Allott	Church	Hayden
Anderson	Clark	Hennings
Bartlett	Cooper	Hickenlooper
Beall	Cotton	Holland
Bennett	Curtis	Hruska
Bible	Dirksen	Humphrey
Bush	Dodd	Jackson
Butler	Dworshak	Johnson, Tex.
Byrd, W. Va.	Engle	Jordan
Cannon	Ervin	Keating
Capehart	Frear	Kefauver
Carlson	Goldwater	Kennedy
Carroll	Gore	Kerr
Case, N. J.	Green	Magnuson
Case, S. Dak.	Gruening	Mansfield

YEAS—72

Martin	O'Mahoney	Smathers
McCarthy	Pastore	Smith
McGee	Prouty	Symington
Monroney	Proxmire	Wiley
Morton	Randolph	Williams, N. J.
Moss	Saltonstall	Williams, Del.
Murray	Schoeppel	Yarborough
Muskie	Scott	Young, Ohio

NAYS—22

Byrd, Va.	Johnston, S. C.	Robertson
Douglas	Kuchel	Russell
Eastland	Langer	Sparkman
Ellender	Lausche	Stennis
Fulbright	Long	Talmadge
Hart	McClellan	Thurmond
Hill	McNamara	
Javits	Morse	

NOT VOTING—4

Bridges	Neuberger	Young, N. Dak.
Mundt		

So the resolution (S. Res. 5) was agreed to.

MR. DIRKSEN. Mr. President, I move to reconsider the vote by which the resolution was agreed to.

MR. JOHNSON of Texas. I move to lay that motion on the table.
The motion to lay on the table was agreed to.*

---

* The motion to reconsider and then to table the motion to reconsider are standard motions giving finality to a vote. The motion having been made and tabled, no Senator may later reopen the question by moving reconsideration.

"Where the Work Is Done"

In a large legislative body which, like the Senate, actively exerts its legislative prerogatives (or, in Senator Muskie's words, treats bills submitted to it as "raw material to be shaped and molded") the major part of the work will be done by committees. Inevitably these will bear the brunt of much of the criticism directed to the parent body. Senator Muskie answers some common criticisms before passing on to a description of committee work.

From his picture of increasing specialization and proliferation emerges a dilemma for which he finds no answer in current proposals for reform. Like most senators, he is committed to the maintenance of a creative role for the Senate in legislation, but the cost of that role is to put the actual control of legislation in the hands of very small groups of senators upon whom the rest must rely for their judgments. It is no longer the Senate as a whole that can create, or even seriously analyze, new policy.

As Senator Mundt emphasizes, the investigating committee is a different type of body from the legislative committee of which Senator Muskie writes. Not all observers would agree with Senator Mundt in his appraisal of this controversy-ridden instrument, but the continued support given Congressional investigations in the annual legislative appropriations would suggest that he reflects an opinion at least widely shared by his colleagues.

X. Committees and Subcommittees in the Senate

Senator Edmund S. Muskie

WHEN PEOPLE OUTSIDE THE CONGRESS COMMENT ON CONGRESsional committees, their initial observations are likely to include at least the following: One, that there are too many of them; and two, that the seniority system gives Southern Senators control of committees and a stranglehold on legislation. As it happens, there is a relationship between these points, and they offer a ground from which to approach an appraisal of the committee and subcommittee system.

Perhaps I may begin with the seniority system. Does it give Southerners the control that is claimed for it? The number of Southern Senators in this context is usually given at eighteen to twenty-two, depending upon how the border states and Texas are counted. Not all of these Southern Senators are chairmen of the standing committees, and in recent years, Northern and Western Senators have been acquiring seniority. For example, Senator Hayden of Arizona is Chairman of Appropriations. Senator Jackson of Washington is Chairman of Interior; Senator Magnuson of Washington is Chairman of Commerce; Senator Anderson of New Mexico is Chairman of Aeronautical and Space Sciences; and Senator Monroney of Oklahoma is Chairman of Post Office and Civil Service.

In my own case, this is my ninth year in the Senate. I am now number four on the Banking and Currency Committee on the Democratic side, number five on the Government Operations Committee, and number three on the Public Works Committee.

On my three standing legislative committees, I have two Southern chairman—Sparkman of Alabama and McClellan of Arkansas—and one Border State chairman, Randolph of West Virginia. I cannot recall a single instance of their blocking a bill from floor action, which a majority of the committee wished to take to the floor, even when the chairman personally opposed the bill.

About the only recent example that I can recall of the stranglehold on legislation is the Judiciary Committee on civil rights, and that stranglehold has been broken by one means or another. In 1965, for example, this was done by the imposition of a deadline by the Senate for the Committee to report back to the Senate on the Voting Rights Bill. In addition, of course, there has been a liberalization of the membership of the Judiciary Committee, with the addition of such junior Northern Senators as Senator Kennedy of Massachusetts, Senator Tydings of Maryland, and others.

Time, age, and recent elections have brought changes in the seniority system and its impact upon the Senate. And it will bring more.

What, then, of the number of committees? I think perhaps a little historical perspective on this would be most useful. In the Senate, the number of standing committees in 1945 was thirty-three. With the Reorganization Act of 1946, that number was reduced to fifteen. Today, in 1967, there are sixteen standing committees, plus two select committees. On the House side, in 1945 the number of committees was forty-eight. In 1946, after the Reorganization Act, it was reduced to nineteen, and today the number is twenty, to which are added two select and two special committees.

But what about subcommittees? In the Senate in 1945, there were thirty-four. In 1950, four years after the Reorganization Act, there were sixty-six. And in 1967, there are 99 subcommittees of the standing committees of the Senate, plus twelve subcommittees of the special and select committees. On the House side, in 1945, there were ninety-seven. In 1950, sixty-five, and today, 141 (including special and select). Obviously the great expansion in the number of committees since the Reorganization Act has been at the subcommittee level. Why? Are there now too many? What impact does this expansion have on the structure and operations of the Senate?

One of the most direct effects of the growth of subcommittees is to lessen the impact of the seniority rule, and this is the point at which the two observations mentioned at the start are related. On my three committees—and this rule probably holds for the other committees of the Senate—only one Senator is chairman of more than one subcommittee. Consequently, relatively junior and non-Southern Senators are chairmen of important subcommittees. Some of these subcommittees have their own budget and their own staff. These are the so-called investigative subcommittees, which must be authorized and given appropriations directly by the Senate. One of my committees, the Subcommittee on Intergovernmental Relations, is classified as an investigating subcommittee; I have my own budget and my own staff, which I control independent of the chairman of the full committee.

These facts give a different perspective on the seniority system and the control which the seniority system is supposed to give to Southern Senators.

Why has there been a growth of the number of subcommittees? The most obvious reason is the increased workload that the Congress has had to absorb since 1946. It is incredible, and it can be measured not only by the growth in number of committees, but growth in Congressional office staffs. Senator Sparkman reminded me once that when he first came to the Senate, which was in the 40's, he had one staff man, in addition to a secretary. The number of staff people a Senator has in his office will vary depending upon how he sets salaries and what his state's allowance is, but in a state the size of Maine, for example, the number can run from thirteen to seventeen staff men in a Senator's office, an indication of the increased workload. This, of course, is reflected also in the number of committees.

The emergence of new problems and new areas of concern in this age of technological and scientific advancement and population growth also requires additional consideration by committees and has led to a growth in subcommittees. Consider the Aeronautical and Space Sciences Committee: At the time of World War II there was no such committee. After World War II, it was established as a minor committee. It has now become a major committee. This is how rapidly new committees can emerge.

Subcommittees also give an opportunity for more in-depth consideration of legislative problems. And this is a reflection of the need for Senators to specialize in particular fields, so that they may more adequately and more effectively enlighten the Senate as a whole in the areas of their specialties. An example is the Air and Water Pollution Subcommittee, of which I am chairman. This is an area in which the federal government's role has grown in the last ten years, and effective public policy depends upon very precise, in-depth knowledge of the technological problems of air and water pollution and of the economic costs. One way of acquiring this expertise and know-how is to establish the subcommittees in which Senators can specialize.

I think at this point I ought to review the specific criticisms about the number of subcommittees.

There is the criticism that it spreads us out too thin. It is not unusual for me to find on my schedule on a morning at least three or four subcommittee hearings or executive sessions going on at the same time, in which I am involved and in which I have a keen interest. But I cannot attend them all.

As a consequence, there is sparse attendance at hearings, which are frequently conducted by a single Senator. This has unfortunate implications: One party and one philosophical point of view are represented; because he is also pressed, the chairman may have to run through the hearing without adequately probing the witnesses' point of view, the witnesses' objection to the legislation or the witnesses' support for it; and too much control over the form and the shape of legislation tends to be placed in too few hands.

In the case of air pollution legislation, for example, the Senate as a whole is likely, after it has tested the validity of my judgments, to accept bills as I and my staff produce them. Fortunately, there are other Senators on the subcommittee who have a keen interest in the field, and so we spread this work out more than may be usual in most subcommittees. But there is increasing control in very few hands over the form and shape of legislation.

Finally, there is the criticism that this proliferation of subcommittees gives too much influence to committee staffs, who are forced to take over from busy Senators in actually drafting the legislation and forming policy recommendations that busy Senators are prone to accept perhaps too quickly and too readily.

There are proposals for reform to reduce the number of subcommittees. First, cut down the number. Second, make them smaller, reducing the number on which any Senator must serve. Third, limit the number of subcommittee chairmanships any Senator can have. I have three. I don't think this is an unusually large number.

The net result of these reforms, if undertaken, would be to reduce the workload of the individual Senator, it is true. But it would also tend to narrow the areas in which he works, and thus narrow the horizon within which he works creatively. These reforms could also result in the neglect of some subject areas of important legislation which the smaller number of committees do not have time to examine. Such suggestions for reforms are mixed in their advantages and disadvantages.

At the present time, proposals are before the Senate for reorganizing or reforming the organization of the Senate and of the Congress as a whole. A great deal of attention has been focused on this particular problem. But frankly, I find it difficult to conceive of ways in which to continue the ability of the Congress to absorb increasingly larger workloads by cutting down on the number of committees with which it can do that job.

Perhaps before proceeding further to a discussion of the effectiveness of the committee system, it would be well to present a few facts about committee structure and membership. The standing committees are divided between so-called "major committees" and "minor committees." Most of them are major. Examples of the "minor committees" are the Committee on Rules and Administration and the District of Columbia Committee. The distinction is not intended to suggest that the work of the minor committees is unimportant, but it does have something to do with the assignment of Senators. Under the Senate rules, a Senator is to serve on not more than two of the so-called major committees, but in addition, he can serve on one of the minor or third committees as they are called.

The number of Senators on committees will vary. The number is larger on major committees than on the minor committees. On the major committees it ranges from about fourteen to twenty-seven. The Appropriations Committee, which has the largest workload of any Senate committee, has the largest number of

Senators. The party division on committees is usually reflective of the party division in the Senate as a whole, although there cannot be an exact comparability. The ratio in the 90th Congress is almost two to one, and committee divisions will not vary from that ratio by more than one Senator either way.

Each of the parties has a slightly different policy on what committee assignments are given to freshmen, although I think they each now strive to give freshmen important committee assignments. President Johnson, when he was Majority Leader, laid down the policy that every new Democratic Senator would be given two important committees. And that has worked ever since. It is a little easier to give Republican Senators important committee assignments because the number involved is so much smaller. It is a little more difficult on the Democratic side.

How effective is the committee system as a legislative function? I remember my initial reaction nine years ago. I was impressed by the amount of work handled by committees. I was impressed by the knowledge and expertise of my senior colleagues. I was impressed by the thoroughness of the job done, both by committee members and by committee staffs, in evaluating legislation. I am still impressed nine years later. I was disturbed nine years ago that there appeared to be too little deliberation in the chamber of this greatest deliberative body on earth, that hard lines of difference were all too frequently automatic, with too little search for accommodation. I think that that initial impression has been sustained all too often, but I think also there have been improvements in this respect, that there is a greater effort made to achieve consensus (perhaps because of the example set in the White House) and to try to accommodate differences.

But rather than generalize about the effectiveness of the committee and subcommittee system and about the methods by which it operates, perhaps I can best describe it in terms of my own subcommittees. These are not necessarily typical, for each subcommittee chairman approaches his responsibilities in his own fashion. A close view of the actual operations of this sample, however, might be more useful than generalizations which would not fit accurately the operations of any existing committee.

My subcommittees are the Subcommittee on Intergovernmental

Relations, the Air and Water Pollution Subcommittee, and the Subcommittee on International Finance. Frankly, I find it stimulating, even though it is time consuming, to be undertaking to work creatively and constructively in such a wide range of fields. It is an educational process for me, that I count as one of the real benefits of service in the Senate. And actually this is one of the products of the seniority system in the Senate which is all too often overlooked. The Senate after all must be a training ground for people who must form public policy in very complicated and delicate fields. They can acquire the ability to do so best by long service in as many subject areas as possible.

How then do I undertake to run these subcommittees? First, we try to learn everything possible about the problems that we are dealing with. We have experts on the subcommittee staffs. As we contemplate hearings which we are to hold, either for the purpose of research or for the purpose of considering specific legislation, I undertake to have the staff do the spadework necessary to give the committee members an initial impression of the problem area in which we are about to work. This staff spadework has produced some notable committee prints, as we call them, of the results of that spadework. We've had this kind of help in the Subcommittee on Air and Water Pollution, where committee prints have found a tremendous demand and commendation outside the Congress. Senator Jackson's Subcommittee on National Policy Machinery has produced committee prints of this kind, which are also in demand. My Subcommittee on Intergovernmental Relations has done the same kind of work. In other words, we take advantage of the expertise in our staff to become acquainted with problems.

Staff spadework involves, of course, digging into the Executive agencies and the Legislative Reference Service of the Library of Congress. Another means used is the questionnaire. For example, in the Intergovernmental Relations Subcommittee, because we are dealing with the problems of the federal system, we are concerned with the points of view of public officials at the levels of local government and state government. Three years ago we sent out an extensive questionnaire, which was developed with the assistance of executive agencies and the Library of Congress, designed to probe the problem areas in the federal system. The results have been published and have been widely used throughout the country, as well as in the Congress.

The second way of educating ourselves on problem areas is by field hearings. In the air and water pollution field, for example, over the past several years we have held hearings from coast to coast. What is the purpose of field hearings? Why don't we stay here in Washington and bring people to us? The reason is, of course, that many of these problems cannot really be understood unless seen where they exist. And water pollution is one of these. Air pollution is another. In addition, in the field we can probe a more representative and broader group of citizens as to their reactions to the problem and what ought to be done.

We conduct hearings in Washington, to which we invite experts to educate us, to teach us. One of the best examples in my experience recently in this area has been in the hearings which my International Finance Subcommittee held in March, May, and August of 1965 on the balance of payments problem. Two volumes of hearings resulted, which have been in great demand throughout the country, not because of what we, as Senators, contributed to them, but because of the knowledge which was made available to us by experts in the government, by experts from the campuses, by experts in the banking field, and by experts from the business field on this problem. They were able to describe the impact of the problem on them and their reaction to proposals for dealing with the international payments deficit.

One other way that we use to probe problem areas is to hold joint hearings with our counterpart committees in the House. I have done this in the case of the Intergovernmental Relations Subcommittee, because there is an Intergovernmental Relations Subcommittee on the House side. We held hearings in 1965 to review the effectiveness of the Advisory Commission on Intergovernmental Relations, which had been created six years before. In this case we were digging for facts, not dealing with specific bills, nor did we conclude that legislation was necessary. Our aim was to probe problems.

This process, even though it is geared primarily at learning, enables us in addition to develop legislative proposals, which are geared to the real and not the imaginary problems. It also enables us to evaluate legislative proposals on a sound basis of fact.

How do we handle moving from the learning process to the actual legislative process? First, we treat the bill before us as raw material. We do not assume because a bill has been introduced, no matter how closely it may be based upon solid advance work, that it is in the form it should take when we are through with it. We treat the bill as raw material to be shaped and molded by our own research and in response to the testimony of witnesses, both favorable and unfavorable, who come before us. We undertake to test the bill against the testimony of witnesses, engaging in colloquy with them, eliciting their sharpest and most precise responses, and undertaking to test our own views against theirs. These meaningful colloquies have been most helpful to us.

In framing legislation we work closely and cooperatively with the Administration—not as rubber stamps, but independently. We rely on the Executive agencies for know-how, for expertise, and for their judgment. At the same time we think we influence changes in their thinking. As testimony to that fact I could offer the history of the recent series of air and water pollution acts: the Clean Air Act Amendments, the Motor Vehicle Air Pollution Control Act, and the Solid Waste Disposal Act of 1965; the Water Quality Act of 1965; the Federal Water Pollution Control Act Amendments and the Clean Water Restoration Act of 1966. All of these were the products of the Air and Water Pollution Subcommittee and initially were not approved by the Administration, but were accepted by it and became part of the Administration's legislative program. The resulting legislation was improved by the differences of opinion between the Administration and the subcommittee, which were resolved in a constructive way.

Thus, we try to work in a creative way with Executive agencies, with our Republican colleagues, with our staff, to achieve reasonable solutions which are geared to as broad a consensus as possible. In addition, we try to develop professionalism and professional standards within the committee itself, within our staff, to complement the research services available to us outside the committee, because we have found that one of the ways to resolve differences and to break down controversies over legislation is to find new drafting techniques for saying what we all would like to see done in a particular bill. Sometimes language can do more to resolve a difference than a philosophic discussion which hides a very real agreement.

Finally, we welcome ideas from any source which will make a bill as precise an instrument as possible for achieving its objectives. I should note that knowing the objectives of the legislation is not as obvious as may appear on the face of it.

Is the legislative process improving? Does the committee system work to move legislation or does it move to hinder it? I know if you probe this question among all members of the Senate you will get many points of view on it. My own view is that whether the committee system moves legislation out to the Senate floor and on to final enactment depends first of all upon whether the country wants action with respect to a particular problem. It depends on whether there is effective leadership in the Executive Branch and in the Congress which is in tune with the country. It does not happen automatically, and I do not think that the committee system can be structured in such a way that it could produce legislation automatically.

The committee system will at times lag behind the mood of the country. At other times it moves with remarkable speed, and at still other times perhaps too fast for the mood of the country. In saying this, I do not want to be interpreted as saying that I think the system is all right as it is. But I am saying that it works, in my judgment, much better than a lot of observers would agree. There are many critics of the Congressional system who are critics because the Congress will not move as fast as they would like; if you probe them, they can't really prove or demonstrate that the Congress is lagging behind the country.

The second question that I think is important to restate here is the question of the seniority system. Does it help or does it hurt, in terms of achieving sound legislation for the country? I have mentioned two criticisms against it: one, that it gives control to the South—a point that I have already analyzed sufficiently to give a basis for judgment; second, that it does not always produce the best leadership of committees. Frankly, I do not know of any alternative that would always produce the best leadership.

The remaining question, as we evaluate the seniority system, is this—should the Chairman of the committee be the choice of the current majority of that committee? In practice, this would mean the current majority of the majority, because the committee chairman obviously would always be chosen by the majority party. One difficulty with that standard is that the current majority of the majority party in a given committee may not necessarily represent the current thinking of the majority of the Senate as a whole. It certainly may not be representative of the country as a whole. In other words, you can find all kinds of holes in any alternative which you can devise to the seniority system.

What then is my personal conclusion? It is that for the most part the seniority system doesn't hurt, although we can all summon up examples proving that it does. I think that the seniority system does operate to produce chairmen who are experienced, who are able, and who are responsive, in most cases, to the will of the majority of the committee.

In conclusion let me summarize the possible areas of reform: (1) the selection of the chairmen of committees; (2) a reduction in the number of committees; and (3) joint hearings, especially for the Appropriations Committees of the two houses. I think this last proposal holds the greatest promise. The appropriations work is the great backbreaking workload of the Congress. There are others, but this, I think all would concede, is the greatest. It absorbs the time of members of both Houses, and of representatives of the Executive agencies. Joint hearings would speed up the process, would shorten our sessions, and would save a great deal of time for members of the Executive Branch, who now must testify before both Houses, as well as for members of the Congress.

There are undoubtedly other areas of reform which will be suggested in the future, as there have been in the recent hearings on legislative reorganization. Nevertheless, I do think that the operation of the committee system as it now stands is substantially different from and better than the impressions which are current even among people who are studying the Congress. It is my hope that this discussion has provided at least a perspective and a better view of it.

XI. The Role of Committee Investigations

Senator Karl E. Mundt

IF THERE IS ONE THING THAT STANDS OUT IN RECENT DIScussions about Congressional investigating committees, it is that they are not well understood by laymen. They are certainly not well understood by people who have never participated in them, and so it is a good thing that we "wrestle with the Devil" in the open a little bit. The committees have been beaten over the head and criticized; that is good. We have learned something from the criticism. But the committees play one of the most important roles in the whole Congressional procedure and the public needs to know more about them.

The misunderstanding about committees shows up in the remarks of outside commentators and would-be reformers of the Congress. We find statements such as one made before the Committee on Government Reorganization a while back by a man who believes that the legislative function of Congress is being so overpowered by Executive domination that the Congress is tending to be a "rubber stamp" institution. He claims that it will either wait for the President to send down a message on, say, labor reform before it legislates on it—sitting around waiting for somebody on high to tell it what to do—or else, if a Member or Senator gets an idea of his own and introduces it, it will be referred to a committee and the committee chairman will refuse to call the committee together until they get a report from the department concerned. "So," he said, "if congressmen degrade themselves to a level where they can only operate sort of at the end of a puppet string from the Administration, let's eliminate the legislative process and make Congress responsible solely for investigations and appropriations!"

Now, this might sound like music to an old-time committee investigator, but it was really a very illogical statement. The solution was wrong even if the criticism was right. Congress has demeaned itself almost unconscionably and has ceased to be a coordinate branch of government in reality, primarily because we have top-heavy majorities and Congressmen who are inclined simply to follow the leadership of some political entity. Thus we reach the point where the committee chairman insists on having a government report before he will have a hearing on a bill and where, before anything is done in a complicated field like labor, we wait for a message from the President.

Now, this is ture, but the answer is certainly not to eliminate the legislative function of the Congress altogether. We should gain a little independence once again. We should develop an attitude in Congress that we are there to legislate, and that the President has every right and duty to propose things, but so do legislators. And if in the end he doesn't like them, he has the veto. That is what the Constitutional founders put it there for. In short, I don't find myself in the camp of the fellow who wants to limit Congressional activities to investigations and appropriations.

At the other end of the spectrum we have textbook writers and critics, commentators from outside, who say we ought to eliminate the investigative functions of Congress. Why in the world is the Congress going around like a bunch of detectives, they say, and trying to investigate things? What do they know about investigation? Why should they be involved in it? That is for the FBI. That is for the Attorney General. That is for the Comptroller General. That is for somebody else. Why the Congress? What do they know about it? What training have they had? And, of course, the answer is none, because you don't get trained for jobs like Senator and Congressman and President and Vice President until you get the job. You have to learn in service. There is a little background that could be helpful, but we are in about the same position as committee investigators—staff people—the first day they are hired. They, too, have to learn on the job.

But I don't find myself in either camp—either with those who think that the investigative function should be *the* great Congressional responsibility along with appropriations, and that alone, or those who say it should be eliminated and that there should not be any Congressional eye watching what is happening in the public sector or, for that matter, in the private sector, when what is happening there affects the public sector.

In the main, I suspect that there are four functions—four duties—of investigating committees. One is to develop the background for legislative change. This is a subject to which I shall return later on with some illustrations, because its importance merits special treatment for it. Here, however, I shall merely list it.

The second function is to examine the degree of conformity that administrators show in meeting the legislative intent. Sometimes when a Congressman or Senator sees how some piece of legislation on which he has worked has been administered by the administrator he is shocked by what has happened to his original concept. He has had an idea; the Congress has accepted the idea; a legislative history has been developed; there is a committee report; there is debate on the floor of the Senate and the House; the bill is passed; the President signs it. Then an administrator is appointed. He interprets it differently than the Senate did. His solicitor makes decisions and spreads out the authority of the act until it is distorted and changed.

A part of the function of the investigative committee is to examine legislative intent and to see that the administrator is doing what he was appointed to do and what he was supposed to do in conformity with the law; not meandering around, not failing to do something, but doing the things he was set up to do. There is a certain latitude for discretion, but the main thrust should be in the direction that is in keeping and in conformity with the legislative intent. The legislation should not be used as a springboard from which to administer a program altogether out of context with what the legislators had in mind when they passed it.

The third purpose of investigating committees is to check on the loyalty and integrity of public officials and employees. We have to have honest people and we have to have patriots in the government, especially in this era of the Cold War. One of the smart tactics which is employed, and understandably so, by our Communist adversaries, is to try to put people loyal to them in our government to confuse us, or to steal our secrets, or to pervert policy, or simply for ordinary old fashioned espionage. So it is important that we have safeguards—with two million and more civilian employees. Some "stinkers" are going to get in. We are supposed to find them. And, when we find them, disclose them or dismiss them or prevent the attainment of the nefarious goals which they seek to achieve.

The fourth main function of the Congressional investigating committee—and there are more that could be mentioned—is to examine the efficiency and effectiveness of administrative operations. It is not enough to have an honest "dope" running a department. It is not enough to have a patriotic, loyal idiot in charge of some governmental operation. There has to be efficiency, too. The taxpayers demand it. The success of our government requires it. How are we going to get it if somebody does not check on it once in a while? Without that check there would be a breakdown in the operation of government, and we might as well be without the laws we have. If some part of the government is not running well, the job of finding out who is responsible cannot be done by looking into a crystal ball. Somebody has to go through the painstaking job of looking at what is being done and finding out what the loophole is. What is wrong? Who is wrong? It may be a perfectly fine, patriotic, honest, decent Sunday school teacher, who simply is not qualified to run that kind of shop.

It is frequently a matter of efficiency, or effectiveness, or of economy—just throwing money away, as the whole controversy over the TFX case involved—not loyalty. Nobody questioned whether McNamara was a patriot or not, or whether he was honest or not, or whether he was a good administrator or not. The question there was: Did he make a wise decision? Over $6 billion was being given to a contractor who was the high bidder instead of the low bidder. We had a responsibility to ask why. Is this economy? Is this efficiency? Was it wise? Was it unwise? We still do not know; we are not prepared to say. But, as a result of the investigation, a lot of corrective measures were taken along the line to tighten up the screens through which these things pass, and some substantial and constructive changes have been made.

The story has not yet been finalized. There was an investigation, but the purpose was not to get anybody dismissed. It was our purpose to check a human judgment on a tremendously expensive contract on which perhaps the fate of the Free World might depend, because if we put that much money into building a weapon that does not work or does not work as well as an adversary's weapon, we are jeopardizing some things pretty precious to us all, and those are freedom and peace and life.

We did not come into the investigation making any charges, and we did not wind up making any charges. We said, "Let's take a look at this thing. It was pretty big. We're kind of curious. How come this most expensive of all contracts goes to the high bidder? How come some civilians, some of whom have never flown a plane, should upset and reverse the unanimous judgment of all of the uniformed user-personnel who examined the statistics?" It was good that we reexamined their thinking. It was good that the questions were asked. When the answer will finally come, I am sure that the country is going to be better off. In short, that is the fourth reason for Congressional investigating committees.

I think that I would agree with Woodrow Wilson when he wrote in his book, *Congressional Government*, that:

> ... Unless Congress have and use every means of acquainting itself with the acts and the disposition of the administrative agents of the government, the country must be helpless to learn how it is being served; and unless Congress both scrutinize these things and sift them by every form of discussion, the country must remain in embarrassing, crippling ignorance of the very affairs which it is most important that it should understand and direct. The informing function of Congress should be preferred even to its legislative function.

With Wilson, I see the congressional investigation as a protective and informational device for the public—the best it has. There isn't any other way that the public would ever have learned about the issues in the TFX controversy. And it learned that it had two sides. It was like the pancake in an Ozark hillbilly's kitchen: It may be awful thin, but never so thin but what it has two sides. This case has two sides. There is the McNamara side; there is the committee side. There is the side of the uniformed services who argue one way, and the civilians and the Pentagon people at the top who argue the other way. But the only way the public is going to learn about it is for somebody to go probing around in an open hearing. To paraphrase another of President

Wilson's well-known sayings: A public decision should be publicly arrived at. One way to do it is to bring it into focus by a congressional investigation.

So far, I have been discussing the functions of investigating committees in terms of the Congress as a whole. But there is another way in which they serve a useful and fundamental purpose so far as the American political system is concerned, and that is as a tool of the minority. If the Senate is, as some would have it, "the most exclusive club in the world," then the minority is surely the most exclusive wing of that club. It has only thirty-six Republican members now, and in my twenty-nine years as a Republican in the Congress, I have been with the majority for only four years.

The two-party system in America is not just a beautiful theory about which to give Fourth of July speeches; it must be a functioning procedure. To have it, the minority needs to have enough authority (and enough people) to put up some kind of debate. It must be able to get the facts out to the people so that it can make an effective argument. The majority can at any time have its way, but if the minority can develop public opinion, perhaps the majority will be more cautious about steamrolling something through. Perhaps it will even change its mind and not pass a particular bill at all. The Senate has given the minority some tools with which to work—such as the protection against sudden cutting off of debate—and the investigative committee is another and very important one.

Nobody likes to be investigated, even when nothing is wrong. It is hard to have to stand up before a television camera and a radio and press gallery and have people presume that you are wrong, even when you know that you are right. You might make a mistake; your memory might go bad. There are lots of things that might be done to embarrass you. But it is one thing to have the investigation a sort of "family reunion," conducted by an administrative agency and another when it is done by a congressional committee and there are two or three minority members there. The investigative committee is a great weapon for the minority, even when that minority is very small.

But to enable the minority to make the best use of it, the investigation must be conducted by experienced members, and with great fairness on the part of the majority and the chairman. Without experience, and without the assurance that the minority will have rights in the investigation, and without trained staff for both the majority and the minority, the investigation will serve no purpose. And public opinion will soon catch up with and discredit any committee which has only Democrats investigating Democrats or Republicans investigating Republicans.

I think that the most horrible example of this was the Bobby Baker investigation. The only time that an investigation occurs in the Senate which is not under the jurisdiction of the Senate Permanent Subcommittee on Investigations is when, by special resolution of the Senate, the matter is given to another committee. This happened in the Baker case because the resolution specified the Rules Committee. The Rules Committee has some very fine Senators on it and is a great committee, but it almost totally lacks experience in conducting investigations. Its members have no expertise at it, and most important of all, it has no trained staff for conducting investigations. Holding and conducting a Congressional investigation without a trained staff is like a mayor trying to maintain order in a city without a trained police force. One cannot get such a staff on sixty days' notice or pick one up out of a bunch of country lawyers, detectives, ex-policemen, and accountants. Most of those that you might find who would be available on such short notice would be individuals whose own work had already been judged not good enough in the private market for such jobs. As it was, the Rules Committee undoubtedly got some fine people, but they were people who had no experience in the special work of Congressional investigation, and very little intimate knowledge about activities and procedures in Washington. They had no expertise in it, no traditions in it, and no experience in it, and neither did the committee members themselves.

The long debate on the Senate floor about the Bobby Baker case brought out some things in the Committee's procedures that were no less than shocking. What was it that the minority members complained about? That the majority refused to let them call witnesses! Had they had a day's experience on an investigating committee, they would have walked out the minute that the majority made that rule, and would have let the public know that they would have no part of such a phony investigation. The public would not have stood still a minute for a one party investigation of that same party's own people. Had the minority members only had the experience to realize this, they would have seen that the Democrats needed them as much as they needed the Democrats in order to hold the investigation, and the minority would have insisted on its basic rights such as the right to call witnesses.

The result was not an investigation at all, but a cat and dog fight between the Republicans and the Democrats, a kind of name-calling contest. As Senator Curtis pointed out, all it really did was to put the finger on people who were so obviously involved that everybody knew about it. It came up with virtually no facts that had not been learned and exposed some place else.

The Permanent Investigations Subcommittee, under Chairman John McClellan, has never had any partisan difficulties of this kind. We have rules of the game—a printed set of rules, which is a good thing to have—and we have a mutual understanding, which is even more important. There are nine members of the Subcommittee: six Democrats and three Republicans. This gives the majority a two to one edge, but the minority has enough, because we require the right to be heard and to assert every right exercised by the majority, and that right is well recognized by the Chairman. We also have a minority counsel who has every right to ask questions from the committee table that the majority counsel has. We have the right to call witnesses, and to question them. And the questions we ask can be embarrassing, or if not embarrassing, they can be the most penetrating questions. That is what they are supposed to be.

While the minority on this committee has the right to call witnesses, I suspect that we do not call, as a minority, one witness out of twenty. This is where the mutual understanding comes in. We talk to "Captain John." We say we think we ought to have this witness and he will agree, and he calls them in due process. But our authority is there. It gives us the power to persuade and to inform, and to bring about the kind of investigation which should take place.

So this is a weapon that the minority has. If you take it away— if you take away the right to call witnesses or to have trained staff or to ask questions in a committee investigation—you no longer have two party government, just as would be the case if you took away the minority's rights in debate.

To return now to the legislative function which was touched on only slightly earlier, this is an area in which investigative committees are frequently criticized. "What legislation have these committees produced?" we are asked. Those who ask simply do not understand the way the Congress is organized. Writing legislation is not the fundamental purpose of an investigating committee. The Congress has legislative committees on every subject in the world. Included in the investigative committee's purpose is the responsibility to find out whether or not there are things which need to be legislated about. It assumes, and should ordinarily assume, that the committee in charge of that area will then come up with the necessary bills.

In one instance in the House, however, during the Alger Hiss case before the House Un-American Activities Committee, a situation came up which was so obvious that Richard Nixon, who was then a member of the committee, and I brought in what was known as the Mundt-Nixon Bill. This bill was enacted by the Congress and became the first seventeen sections of the Internal Security Act of 1950. In this case the investigation by the committee brought out so dramatically some weaknesses in our security system that the committee itself came up with a proposal that has become the law of the land.

A somewhat different case, but one which illustrates more nearly the kind of relationship between investigations and legislation that I am trying to describe, is shown by the Landrum-Griffin Act, which was a direct outgrowth of the labor racket hearings held by the Senate Investigations Committee. Our committee held long hearings, and after they were all through, came up with a report saying that there ought to be legislation to take care of certain conditions. We who were on the committee did not believe, in the main, that there was anything wrong with the union movement in this country that democratization of it would not cure, but new legislation seemed necessary to correct certain abuses. We brought this kind of information out in our report, suggested the general outline of bills, tossed in a couple of bills with McClellan and Mundt co-authorship—because we were the ranking members of our investigating committee—to dramatize what we had in mind, and retired from the arena.

Then the Labor Committees of the Senate and the House, properly having jurisdiction, took our suggestions, took the hearings, took the report, and held additional hearings to a legislative end. They produced the Landrum-Griffin Act, but its origins lay in our work, and it came as a direct result of the investigation which was carried out by our committee. Later, of course, McClellan and I helped bring about passage by participating in the debate on the Senate Floor.

Before closing, there are two other controversial aspects of investigative committee work that deserve brief mention: the fairness of committee procedures and the question of televised hearings.

Are Congressional investigations fair to witnesses? Do innocent people get injured? It certainly could not be claimed that an innocent person never gets injured in a Congressional investigation. Innocent people are accidentally injured everywhere. But there is no pattern of injury to innocent people in committee investigations, and many effective safeguards have been established to protect innocent individuals.

When I was Acting Chairman of the House Committee on Un-American Activities during the time of the Alger Hiss case, when the elected chairman, J. Parnell Thomas, was otherwise unhappily engaged, the first thing I did was to ask the Brookings Institution to develop a set of suggested rules of procedure. Of their recommendations—on which they did a good, workmanlike job—we took about 80 percent and adopted them by committee resolution. These still provide the hard core of the book of procedures used by the House Committee on Un-American Activities and by the Senate investigating committee, which is the oldest one in the business. These procedures are set up to protect the witness; they are set up to give the committee the right to get the facts; and they are set up to give the members of the majority and the minority their respective roles to play.

In all honesty, I would much rather be a witness before a Congressional committee under those rules of procedure than to be a witness in a court of law under the rules of jurisprudence which prevail there. As one example of my reasons for this, consider the situation of a witness in a court of law: The lawyer questioning him asks, "Were you in your home at nine o'clock this morning? Yes or no?"

The witness replies, "Well, I'd like . . ."

"Answer yes or no."

"Could I talk to my attorney?"

"No. Answer yes or no."

If the witness refuses to answer, the judge can hold him in contempt, and he will go to jail.

What happens to the same fellow before an investigating committee? First of all, he is not in a witness box with his lawyer across the room from him; his attorney is sitting by his side. If the committee asks the witness a tough question, he may consult his attorney before answering. If the committee doubts his answer, it may threaten him with prosecution for perjury, but, again, he may consult his attorney then and there, and decide what he should do. This is a tremendous advantage for a witness.

I think, perhaps, we may have gone a little too far in granting this sort of protection, but it is there, and it is just one illustration of the rules of procedure as they operate before investigating committees to protect innocent people.

The other question was whether hearings should be televised. For myself, I see no reason why a hearing which is open to the public—and that means the press, the photographers, and ultimately the cinema newsreels—should not be open to radio and television also, so long as they behave themselves. The lights are a little hot. It is a little difficult looking in them sometimes. It is a little uncomfortable for the people at the committee table. But why should not a fellow who lives in South Dakota have the same access to public business as the citizen of nearby Virginia or Maryland, who can walk into the committee room every day and watch his government perform? Television just rolls back the walls, flattens them out, and lets the people in South Dakota and every other state have the same right as the people in the District of Columbia to visit the committee room. To keep television out is to hold selective open hearings—open only to those who can commute in—which seems to me to be an indefensible position.

The argument that television bothers a witness is meaningless, especially if all he is going to do is say, "I take the Fifth

Amendment." He can say that on television as well as without it. After all, any type of hearing "bothers the witness." The same argument on that score to eliminate television could be used to eliminate newsmen, photographers, committee recorders—and, eventually, the hearings themselves. On the rare occasions when a witness is found who is jittery, nervous, or upset, and who is willing to cooperate, but has never been in front of television before, the committee will and does have the lights turned out and the cameras turned off, provided he does in fact cooperate and testify. As for the criminal who is going to take the Fifth in any case, let the lights show him up! If the committee knows all about him, and knows he has made a career of crime, perhaps it will save some future victim to know his face and to know what kind of nefarious character he actually is.

Perhaps the best way to conclude this discussion is with a text—and for this, I have chosen the words of J. Edgar Hoover, a man most Americans very highly respect, whether or not they always agree with him, and who is surely more knowledgeable about the investigative machinery than any other man in this country. Speaking before the special committee to investigate organized crime in interstate commerce, he said,

> I know of no other force in American life that can render such a salutary service as the Congressional investigative committee in exposing conditions which are inherently evil. The broad powers vested in such committees give them opportunities not available to the usual investigative process.

There lies behind this statement a little known fact, and a most important one: The investigative committee has authority and power that the FBI does not have, and that we should not wish it to have. The FBI cannot subpoena a witness; the committee can. It can subpoena anybody from Cabinet members on down. It cannot make them talk—they can plead executive privilege or take the Fifth Amendment—but they must come before us with their papers. If they fail to testify truthfully, or if they plead the Fifth Amendment when it does not apply, the committee can have them prosecuted for perjury or require them to appear in court for contempt of Congress.

The FBI cannot do that. It can arrest a suspect, but it cannot make him answer, nor jail him for perjury if he lies. Nor would we want the FBI to have such a power; that would change it into a Gestapo. These powers the Congressional committees have because they use them in the open. The FBI operates under cover as a detective agency must. In the words, again, of J. Edgar Hoover speaking of congressional investigating committees, "We need this supplementary force for us to do the job and the country needs it for its own benefit."

I conclude by summarizing: We need the investigating function of Congress to protect our freedom and to promote and preserve the best results obtainable in this self-governing Republic.

The Problem of Ethics

For the man in public life, ethics is not solely a matter of individual or private behavior. As Senator McCarthy shows, it is a central consideration in the decisions he must make on behalf of the people and the nation he represents. Public policy is a matter of value choice, establishing authoritatively those patterns of conduct which not only individuals, but the political system itself should follow.

Shortly after Senator McCarthy's essay was written, the Senate was faced with the necessity of passing upon the behavior of one of its members in a realm which mingled the public and the private. A Select Committee on Ethics and Conduct, of which Senator McCarthy was a member, brought in a resolution of censure against Senator Thomas J. Dodd of Connecticut. Senator Dodd was accused by the Committee of diverting the proceeds of testimonial dinners (allegedly given as campaign fund-raising events) to his own use and of billing both the Senate and private organizations for expenses on several trips.

Important issues were raised by the case.

Senator Dodd had used the proceeds of his dinners to maintain a standard of life which was apparently well above the average for Americans, but do not the political and social pressures of Washington life seem to demand such a standard? Is there a danger that public office can become, as the Senator asks, "the exclusive domain of the wealthy?" Is the cost of our privately-financed political campaigns, on which the Senator also rested his case, too great to allow a man of modest means to compete without severe temptation to either this type of behavior or to the incurring of obligations that would lead to a conflict of interest? (It may be noted in passing that conflict of interest charges against Senator Dodd had also been considered by the Committee, but that it had found the issues too complex and the evidence too uncertain to act upon.)

Senators Brooke and Tower presented the issue of due process. In this, the Senate was caught in a web of its own making. Never having established a code of conduct, could it with justice punish a *member for improper conduct? The Committee felt that it could, and in the final vote, the Senate agreed.*

In the end, there remains a question whether or not justice was either the object or the outcome of the case. Although it was Senator Dodd who faced the accusations, it was the Senate itself, in Senator Moss's words, which was on trial. The members were clearly acting under the pressure of public opinion. Having finally censured Senator Dodd on one of the counts of the charge, the Senate virtually apologised to him. The Majority Leader, in his remarkable closing speech, called him "friend and colleague." This language can hardly be dismissed as lacking in significance. The Senator had been censured for a course of conduct which had "brought the Senate into disrepute," as Senator Stennis stated in his opening charge. Was it the Senate itself that stood convicted?

The selections from the censure debate given here neither portray its character nor summarize it. Rather, they are a sampling of its more lucid moments. It was not a good debate. As if to avoid facing the difficult task of judging their colleague, the Senators turned first upon his accusers, columnists Drew Pearson and Jack Anderson, and berated them in terms more severe than any they used against Senator Dodd. (Pearson and Anderson had broken the case by the use of documents copied or taken from Dodd's files by disaffected employees without the Senator's knowledge.) The defense was by turns emotional—often to the extent of visibly embarrassing Senator Dodd himself—and trivial in its picking over small items in the statistics supporting the charge. Most of these aspects have been omitted from the portion here given.

XII. Congressional Ethics

Senator Eugene J. McCarthy

THESE ARE VERY UNHAPPY TIMES FOR MORALISTS, OR SO I gather from the comments of some of the professionals in the field of moral and ethical philosophy. The problems of choice, of decision, and of discrimination are difficult, even for those whose lives are dedicated to the problem of right and wrong and the judgment as to methods and means. Consequently, it is appropriate to ask for some understanding of the problems of politicians, whose role is of a somewhat lower order than that of the moralists and philosophers in that we are called upon to take what they may propose as a compromise and apply it in the very real world.

My topic, then, is a perplexing one. To deal with it, my remarks will be about two general areas: first, the relationship of ethics to politics as it bears upon the action of members of the United States Senate and, for that matter, the House of Representatives or the President or anyone in government; second, the more limited question of morality of the individual person in government. The first part deals with the larger conception of ethics and the pursuit of justice. The second part treats matters of honesty and of integrity in office.

Politics is not a simple extension of ethics, but it does depend upon ethics, philosophy, and other disciplines. It does so for two purposes: first, for the determination of its objectives and goals. Politics is not a self-contained discipline or a self-contained science, and generally when any political system claims this kind of completeness for itself, the consequences are disastrous to the people. This has been the case in totalitarian political philosophies or systems where this confusion does occur. Secondly, politics is dependent upon ethics to establish standards for judging the methods and the means used in government and political life.

Politicians, therefore, should be moralists. If they cannot be or if they feel that they are limited, they ought to seek advice and counsel from those who are somewhat more learned and somewhat more attentive to this particular discipline. It is reported that medieval rulers carried moral theologians to consult and to advise them. Today we do not follow that practice. Most of us carry an economist instead.

There is in the United States—and not only in the United States—a disposition to over-moralize issues. In the course of campaigns we are disposed to present our case under the name of a crusade. This is especially true of those who are out of power and are challenging those who are in power. They assert that their approach to political problems will be non-political, which is really a contradiction in terms, and insist that their approach will be different: that it will be a moral and a spiritual one. Often it is said at the same time that if men were really of good will, if there were only good people in government, we would then come up with the right answers. The difficulty about these approaches is never discovered until those who advocate them are elected to office. At that point they have to face up to some rather hard decisions. If they sit down together to consider the problems and are not able to come up with the right decisions, then they have to admit either that not everyone in the government is a man of good will—and that would be a hard decision to make—or that their theory is not right. In other words, it is not possible to approach a political problem as though it were simply a moral and a spiritual one. It is necessary to identify the proper area of politics and the kind of political decisions which have to be made.

The role of politics is a practical one of the determination and application of ways and means. In its purest form, politics is concerned with bringing about progressive and orderly change in keeping with the demands of justice. Justice is the objective for society generally and certainly the objective of political action. But the immediate and the primary objective is to establish an order which, by whatever definition of justice, and whatever elements we think go into a definition of it, can be defined as progressive change.

There are times, however, when men in office, public leaders, and officials of parties in power, do not have this kind of simple and positive choice which will bring about progressive change and improvement. Sometimes the decision, the right decision, the good decision, the decision for which they should be given full credit, might be one which simply holds things as they are. There are periods in history, in the history of nations, and certainly in the history of the world in our own generation, in which men of great good will and great wisdom would have to be given full credit for simply having stabilized things or in some cases even to have slowed down the rate of retrogression towards a kind of barbarous society. In this somewhat relative world of political decisions a fair judgment of politicians, of administrations, of parties in power, of any responsible government authority, must be made against a background of history and of current forces, taking into account the real world in which the simple choice between that which is altogether good and that which is altogether bad is seldom offered and in which most choices have to be made somewhat in between these two extremes.

Edmund Burke, in one of his essays, said that the number of forces or factors bearing upon any political decision is infinite and that consequently the number of possible decisions, each of which might be justified, could also be infinite. This is, I suppose, the extreme presentation of the problem and, perhaps, the easiest presentation or attempt to present standards by which political decisions may be judged.

In the Congress of the United States the compromises which are called for are of several varieties.

You may be called upon to compromise with what you would consider to be a principle. Let us take the question of civil rights, which is the most pressing moral problem and most pressing political problem which faces our nation today. Members of the Senate from southern states could be quite convinced themselves that segregation was politically and morally wrong and that it was entirely contrary to the Constitution of the United States and to the traditions of our land, and that this was a fundamental question of principle. One might ask: how can they justify an accommodation or a compromise in, let us say, voting against a civil rights bill as most of them have in the past? Their justification, and I think this is true in most cases, has to run somewhat to this end: that this is an issue on which they would be wholly unable to persuade their constituency if they were to stand forth. So they move on from that to the second question: what would happen if they were defeated because of a stand on this issue, what kind of person would then come to the United States Senate or the United States Congress? They conclude he would be as bad or worse on this particular issue, but he would probably be bad on almost every other issue on which the Congress might be called upon to act. A member would not have to take this compromising position, but I say it could be an entirely moral and a proper and a prudent decision for him to take. He might also decide that the issue was of such overriding moral importance and that it was a principle of such great consequence he would say, "I'm going to vote for it anyway, and take the consequences," a kind of willingness to make himself a political martyr. Well, again this might be a defensible action. It would depend upon whether he had judged wisely that the time for this kind of defeat, this kind of martyrdom, had really arrived. It might turn out that this was a very bad decision, if the man who succeeded him was so bad or if the issue was so stirred up in his own state that the condition of that state became worse than before. You could judge him as a politican in the light of that harsh standard. I would say, "Here is a great man," because he took this clear stand. He might be a great man. But you would have to hesitate to say, "Here is a great politician," because he took this stand. That judgment would depend upon the consequences of it in terms of his own state or in terms of what might happen in the Congress or in the nation. One could take this position. However, if a man who represented a state of this kind was convinced in principle that segregation and discriminatory practices were bad, he would certainly not be justified in making extreme statements even though they represent the views of his constituents. He would be under obligation to play it most carefully and most quietly and with as great as possible restraint. But here is a question of principle which could quite justifiably require compromise and concession—a retreat from the pure position.

A second case is that in which it is necessary to make a choice between what might be called two principles. We had experience with reference to this in civil rights matters in the past before we enacted the comprehensive bill in 1964. Before that time, on almost every issue involving any kind of social benefit, housing or education or medical benefits or hospital construction, it was not at all uncommon to have some member offer civil rights amendments. I would not say that in every case they acted in good faith, because sometimes they offered amendments relating to civil rights when they were opposed to the basic bill to which they were offered, expecting thereby to weaken and possibly to defeat the original bill. Let us take an education bill to which a civil rights amendment is offered. Members of the Congress would then have to make this kind of choice involving an ethical position. If they were persuaded that the addition of the civil rights rider would have the effect of killing the education bill, then they might decide to vote against that amendment so that the education bill could be passed. You have to make a kind of determination as to which principle is more important at this time, to make this decision in the light of your best judgment about the current movement of civil rights legislation, the disposition of the Senate and the Congress itself, and whether greater good might come for America through the passage of an education bill without a civil rights rider. This is a case of choice between two positions, each of which involved a position of principle.

The third kind of compromise is one which is usually somewhat easier to make. It has to do with degree, the question of taking something less than one might like. This sort of compromise occurs on almost every major controversial piece of legislation that comes before the Senate, certainly on almost every appropriation. It has been the case with reference to the protection of voter rights over the past several years during which these rights have been under debate.

Another area of compromise which we are called upon to make is that of deciding at what point the government should not take action, should not intervene, should not attempt to lay down laws or to seek procedures for enforcement. Here again you reach an area in which the line cannot be clearly drawn. It is a vague and fluid line. We can lay down some rather general principles that really government should not seek to direct or control the morality of the people in those things which are essentially private and which do not have any clear or definable public consequence, that is, consequence in terms of those things which are considered necessary to civic life. We could go beyond that, and say these have somewhat serious consequences in terms of family life, for example. But, unless a clear case can be made that the civic life itself is definitely and positively being undermined, the general rule should be that government should refrain—should stand aside. Government may take action to eliminate the conditions which lead people to acts that are somewhat destructive of the normal public good, but to move affirmatively and positively and with great strength into each and every one of these areas would be a perversion of government. The compromise takes place in the in between area. A rather good line about this occurs in Shakespeare's principal play of political philosophy, *Measure for Measure*. After the prince has gone out to have a look at the world, he comes back and he is asked, "What's abroad in the world?" And he said, "There is so great a fever on goodness, that the dissolution of it must cure it." A disposition to eliminate everything that was bad was what he had observed, and his conclusion was that if this goes on, the whole structure of society will be destroyed.

One final area which might be called ethical compromise, or at least for which basic and profound ethical judgments are called for, is in the field of foreign policy. I suppose in some ways this is the most difficult area of choice today, one in which the President and his advisers are more intimately and more deeply involved than are the members of the Senate. But because under the Constitution the Senate has a special responsibility for foreign policy and because foreign policy in a society such as ours is a kind of projection of the intellectual and the moral judgment of the people, all of us do bear some responsibility for those decisions.

We do often have men in high places in government who believe, as one said recently, that in the conduct of our international propaganda program we should proceed with no holds barred as though we were fanatics and with no questions asked.

More recently a man in a similar position in the Department of Defense spoke of the right of the government to lie to the people. Perhaps this was out of context to some extent—anytime you quote one sentence it is out of context. But he did say it, and even in context, there was enough in it to cause us to run up a flag of caution and ask just what is really meant by this.

We hold in this country that national interest, national self-interest, is not overriding. It does not justify every action that may be taken by our government. If we do not believe this then we certainly have no justification and no right for the strength which we gave to the Nuremburg trials and to our participation in them. So we are very clear on the record—not just in terms of what we have said, but also in the cases of our support of international law and the application of it in a number of instances—demonstrating that we do not accept that we or any nation can act without restraint, on the basis that this action or this order advances the national interest.

Diplomacy and decisions on international affairs call for the application of moral judgment, first of all, because we live and act under the shadow of and the potential of the great destructiveness of nuclear weapons. Secondly, because at no time in history has the concern for the decent opinion of mankind—that concept first stated in the Declaration of Independence—been as important and necessary and real as it is today. In 1776 the decent opinion of mankind, if it could have been discovered, involved only a few million people who might have been concerned, or whose judgment might have had some bearing upon this revolutionary action here on the North American continent. But today the decent opinion of mankind comprehends almost everyone in the world. When President Johnson addressed the Joint Session of Congress in 1964 on the question of voting rights, he invited the ambassadors of all the countries represented in the United States. There were some who said that this is really a strange action. Why should he invite the ambassadors to come in and sit with us while he talks about what is really an American, a domestic problem? I think the explanation is rather clear; that the problem of discrimination and segregation in the United States is no longer just a domestic problem. Certainly it is no longer just a problem for Alabama and Mississippi and Louisiana as we held for nearly 100 years. It is a problem for the whole United States but beyond that it is a problem for the entire world. The concern for the decent opinion of mankind has become more important not just in a quantitative sense but in terms of intensity and quality, and so we need to be concerned about the ethical and the moral justification of the actions which we take.

The second area dealing with ethics and morality which I wish to discuss here is the more limited one of morality in government. I made the distinction at the beginning that in this area I am not referring to broad ethical judgments—about justice and about world peace and setting up standards by which our statements to the world may be judged or our military action may be judged. Rather, I have in mind the more personal problem of how should a man in public office—a member of the Senate or member of the House of Representatives—conduct himself. Perhaps we might touch on how they do conduct themselves, although this is a kind of personal judgment which I hesitate to make on any member of the Congress of the United States.

Peter Odegard, writing in 1937 in the *Encyclopaedia of the Social Sciences* on the question of corruption, said that the level of morality among public officials in the United States was the worst of any in the world at that time. I do not know whether he really knew whether this was an accurate statement or not, and I am not prepared to say whether there has been any great improvement since that time. I do think that there has been some improvement at every level of government: the level of local government, the level of state government. I would hesitate to say that there has been great improvement at the federal level because I do not think the measure of corruption at the federal level was ever comparable to that in local and state governments. You could make a comparison between the Harding administration and the conduct of government in the last two or three administrations and say that there is nothing comparable in these administrations to what took place in that, but because that was a more or less isolated case, it was not a reflection of a trend or of a general prevailing condition and I do not think the comparison is actually very valid. In any case we need to be concerned continuously about the personal moral standards of men who hold public office in a democracy. Whatever that level may be, I think it is a reflection of three general forces that bear upon it.

One is the general level of morality which exists in the country. This will be transferred and demonstrated by those who hold public office, in part because they come from that kind of moral background and moral climate and will carry it into the conduct of their offices, and also because there can be a transfer to them from the people; that is, under certain circumstances you might have a man whose personal ethics and morality were somewhat higher than those of his constituents, but who might be moved to compromise and to hedge, reflecting the disposition, the attitudes, and the practices of his own people. On occasions we have been called upon at least in the press to discipline members of the House or the Senate because of actions which are really outside the Congress itself: moral faults, dishonesty, whatever it may be. We have had men elected to Congress while they were serving in the federal penitentiary for violation of federal income tax laws and other laws.

It is very difficult for the Senate or the House to take such action. If we were to begin to move to lay down standards, at least after an election was over, it could lead to very severe limitations upon who might run for office or who might be admitted once he was elected. The general disposition is to say that the people of a district or of a state are called upon to pass this kind of judgment, and that once they have made it, the Congress should accept the judgment of the people if the particular member does not violate the rules of the Senate or the House and if he conducts himself within those rules; what he may have done outside or what he may do outside is subject to review by his own constituency and, of course, by the courts when he offends personally. This is an area into which we should not easily or quickly intrude.*

There is a second influence which I think is more direct and, perhaps, more significant, and that is the influence of the standards of morality which are accepted in those professions or in the business community that touch most directly upon politics. Since a majority of members of Congress are drawn from the legal profession, you can expect that the ethical and moral standards of that profession will be reflected in the kind of men who

* The foregoing was written before the House of Representatives took action in the Adam Clayton Powell case. The immediate re-election of Powell after the House vote to deny him his seat would seem to illustrate the problems involved.—ED.

hold public office. To the extent that those standards are high, that those standards are good, then you will have a comparatively high level of morality in the Congress itself. If the level of morality in the business community is high and if they are concerned not to currupt men in public office, then there would be a kind of one-to-one or at least a direct relationship between the level of morality in the business community—which does touch very directly and is intimately involved in politics—and the level of morality in public office itself.

Mr. Dooley said by way of defending public officials (most of his experience was in Chicago, but this may have more universal application) that he had never known a politician who was corrupted, excepting by a businessman. I do not mean to blame the businessmen, but to make this point of transfer and of the direct bearing of the level that exists in those professions, in business, and in those activities which are close to politics.

And thirdly, of course, the level of morality in politics and government will be a reflection of the general attitude toward public office itself. Here one is forced to make some rather broad historical judgments. I think it fair to say that in consequence of the Revolution, or the philosophy that went with it, there came the rejection of the idea of any kind of aristocracy or any kind of special claim that might go with one's birth or one's family or with one's position to public office. We may have lost, or at least we have not quite carried over or transferred or developed, the necessary sense that public office itself carries very special kinds of responsibility and very special obligations.

I think that most members of the United States Senate and most members of the Congress are sensitive to the special obligations and the special responsibilities of that office. I do think it important that we continue to stress and to emphasize that public office in a democracy, particularly, carries with it the same kind of obligations that in earlier and somewhat simpler times were attached to birth and to title. It is significant that in recent years whenever a person holding public office was called upon to justify what was judged by many to be improper action, he was inclined to justify it in terms of what was accepted in the profession from which he came—for example, that within the legal profession taking a fee of a certain kind was quite in order. And he could have been quite right, entirely legal, and entirely in order. He might say that in the business world such and such a practice is an acceptable practice and again he could have been quite right—not just a legal practice but even morally acceptable. But there has been little or no realization that as he moved from that order into the world of public office, the special responsibilities and the special duties of office carried with them this additional burden of a more refined and more particular moral responsibility. You may recall one man a few years ago who said he had done nothing but what his mother would have approved. It seemed like the ultimate defense, but really it just opens the question as to what his mother really believed. She might have been a very good woman, but she may very well not have had an understanding of the special obligations and the special duties that went with the office which he held.

If, then, we want to raise the level of morality of public officials, these three things, I would say, are needed:

First, to raise the general level of morality in the country.

Secondly, to continue the effort to raise the level of morality in the business and the professional world. I would note that I think there has been a great improvement here. The legal profession is a long-standing profession and has continuously been concerned about ethics in the Bar and before the Bar, but most encouraging, I think, have been the signs of a new sense of moral obligation and of concern for the public good in the business community of America. And this has come, I think, fortunately at a time when there has been a greater and greater concentration of power in the large corporations of this country. I would cite just two examples: the response of the business community without any real legal pressure in the postwar period with regard to profit taking and to pricing policy when persuaded either by their own reflection or, in one or two cases, with some encouragement from the government. They responded, and it was not just a response to pressure or to the man. More recently—although I am not so sure their judgment is good in this case—they responded to the Presidential request that they cut down on their investments in European countries, for the most part in the interest of preserving our gold supply and doing something about the balance of payments; in this case I think there is some mistake in their practical judgment, but I think the response is an indication of good will, and it is a moral response on their part.

The third and vital necessity is our continuous attention to raising the level and the sensitivity of men in public office to the special burdens and the special obligations that do go with public office. We can do something with codes and with directives. They can set limits and they can set guidelines and give direction. But I think it would be a great mistake for us to believe that in dealing with the chosen representatives of the people—the House and the Senate—that you can set rather narrow directives in lines which are to be used either in making the choice or which should give direction to the conduct of the man in public office. There is in any representative democracy, and certainly in ours, that point where you have to make the hard and difficult decisions, where all of the forces really somehow come together; and we have really found no better way to do it than to elect men to a representative body—to the Senate and to the House in the case of the United States—and also to elect a President. This involves a commitment in trust to them, reserving the right, of course, to a periodic review: two years for House members and four years for a President and six years for the United States Senate. So ultimately in the case of the conduct of members of the Senate and of the House and of the President, guidelines and directives and codes can have only a limited effect. The real test will come in a sense of moral dedication and moral obligation on a personal basis, but beyond that to the extent that each understands the full measure of the responsibility of his own office.

XIII. The Dodd Censure Resolution Debate*

MR. STENNIS† . . . THE OVERALL NATURE OF THIS CHARGE IN the resolution is not a general condemnation of testimonial dinner as such. It does not base any charge against the Senator from Connecticut because of a testimonial dinner or any other kind of dinner—just the fact that it was held. The basis of the charge is on the use of the money collected. That is the sole basis of the charge.

There is no attempt to convict him of violating Federal law, Connecticut law, or any other law, or failing to pay income tax or failing to file a report. This goes solely to the use of the money. This is money collected under all the banners and trappings of campaign expenses, past or future, especially so far as the public was concerned, and then a great part of it was spent indiscriminately for personal use and personal debt. That is the basis of the charge. . . .

The words used in the charge itself are "course of conduct." It amounted to a course of conduct that was wrong on its face, and therefore brought the Senate into disrepute. . . .

I want to make a brief reference here to the power and authority of the Senate to pass on alleged misconduct of Members.

The Senate possesses two kinds of power, one supplementing the other, which relates to prescribing rules of conduct for its Members and the disciplining of Members for misconduct.

First, the Senate, being a sovereign and continuing body, has inherent power to insist upon and maintain moral and ethical

*Congressional Record, June 13–23, 1967, pp. S8079–S8723.
† As Chairman of the Select Committee on Ethics and Conduct, it was Senator Stennis' duty to present the case against Senator Dodd.—ED.

standards in its own house. Second, it has express constitutional power to do so. . . .

There are no written rules—even though that has been done—for expulsion. There are also no written rules, gentlemen, for testing a person's right to take his seat in the Senate as a Member.

Senators may be surprised to know that there are a few provisions in the Corrupt Practices Act, enacted about 1926, which have some bearing upon that question. But there are no prescribed rules of conduct written out in advance that would affect a Senator in the matter of taking his seat. Still such proceedings of this kind have been instituted at least 150 times, and carried through to a decision in many of those cases during the history of the Senate. . . .

So there is nothing novel about this particular situation which faces the Senate. Our major jurisprudence is based upon the unwritten rules of equity courts, which are courts of conscience, as we lawyers say. This case being presented is a matter of conscience, ethics, and conduct, pertaining not merely to one Senator, but to how it affects the Senate. . . .

Members of the Senate, [the] facts are not in dispute.

The conclusions and the purposes are in dispute, but [the] facts are largely admitted in [the] stipulations by Senator Dodd and the committee.

From all the evidence of Senator Dodd's direct and indirect control of the organization and administration of the several fundraising events conducted from 1961 through 1965, from the recurring patterns of notice and so forth to the public of the purpose of each of these events, and notwithstanding this notice, the conversion to his personal purpose of substantial parts of the proceeds from each fundraising event, as well as from funds contributed to his election campaign, there emerges an inescapable conclusion that unfortunately the Senator from Connecticut deliberately engaged in this course of conduct to divert to his own use funds over which he held only a trustee or fiduciary control.

There is another item here that I have not discussed, and that is the so-called double billing. That item is going to be discussed in detail by others.

The committee made a very careful examination of these matters, Members of the Senate, and I have here a statement about them. These duplicate travel payments are covered on page 23 of the committee report, and I will now read that in the *Record*. It reads:

> On seven occasions from 1961 through 1965, Senator Dodd, while traveling on official Senate business, paid for by the Senate, also received substantially equivalent expense reimbursement for the same transportation from private groups for his appearance as a speaker at various events (pp. 746, 747, 863–865, Hgs.). . . .

REPLY TO THE ETHICS COMMITTEE REPORT

MR. DODD. Mr. President, I thank the Presiding Officer. Let me say to the distinguished majority leader that I have no interest in delaying these proceedings. I have had none. The sooner they are concluded, the better I shall feel. . . .

I come before you to present my response to the recommendation of the Senate Ethics Committee that I be censured on two counts—that I diverted political funds to personal use, and that I was guilty of deliberately billing the Government for travel for which I was paid from other sources.

It is you, the Members of the Senate, who will be my final judges, and it is to you that I address my appeal.

A man's reputation is his most precious possession. And for a Senator who values his reputation there could be no prospect more ruinous than the condemnation or censure of his peers. It is tantamount to a capital offense conviction from which there is no appeal.

It is my hope, therefore, that in weighing my case the Members of the Senate will attempt to assess the fundamentals as well as the details; that I will enjoy the presumption of innocence to which every accused man is entitled; that, where conflicting testimony results in doubt, I will be accorded the benefit of the doubt; that the issues will be decided only on their merits, and that political considerations will not be permitted to intrude on this decision.

In appealing against the recommendation of the Ethics Committee, I do not challenge their integrity or their fairness. In the course of my Senate duties, I have learned to know them all and to respect them all.

But even the wisest and fairest of judges and examiners are fallible; and it is the recognition of this basic fact that makes the right of full evidentiary review an essential and frequently employed component of our system of jurisprudence....

I know that my personal tribulations and my emotional response to these tribulations bear no relevance to the charges against me. But I would, nevertheless, like to say something on this subject, because I feel it will enable you to better understand the difficulties I have experienced in coping with this situation.

I am sure the situation I confronted has its counterpart in the personal experience, at one time or another, in one degree or another, of every one of you, of every man and woman in the land.

Is there anyone alive who has not felt in some—perhaps fleeting—moment of anguish, that goodness has suddenly fled the world? That all of the canons of justice have been repealed? That the minimum requirements of human decency have been suspended? A moment, I mean, when, without deserving it, you come under general attack; when you know the attack is unjust, yet others deny or doubt what you know....

I was taught that one lives with the record when proving or disproving a case.

Perhaps my position would have been better understood if I had kept my personal funds and my testimonial funds carefully separated from each other, and if I had used my testimonial funds exclusively for the purpose of liquidating my political debts and covering, or partially covering, my unreimbursed costs of office....

Perhaps my office bookkeeping procedures could have been improved. Indeed, in retrospect I am prepared to concede that the bookkeeping that went on in my office was incrediably sloppy in many ways. For this I do not seek to divest myself of responsibility....

I am responsible—but, Mr. President, I am not guilty. By any honest accounting I have not profited one penny from public office.

Mr. President, the implications of this case go far beyond what happens to me or my family.

A question at issue is whether men of moderate means are to

be able to compete for office, or whether public office is to become the exclusive domain of the wealthy.

A question at issue is whether we are here to enshrine a precedent which makes ex post facto justice permissible when Senators come before Senate committees to defend themselves against charges that have been made against them.

A question at issue is whether a Senator so defending himself is entitled to the same protection of due process as a citizen who comes before a court of law.

A question at issue is whether freedom of the press involves the right of muckraking columnists to conspire to steal the files of any public official or private citizen they dislike.

If this kind of thing is allowed to go uncalled, unpunished, no office in this Capitol, no office in this city, no public office throughout this land will be safe from the same sort of thing that was done to me. No one. The word will go out, "We have a license to steal, particularly from a public official."

Let no one say that the means do not matter. As Justice Douglas said in a cogent statement addressed to every American:

> The means are all important in a civilized society. It may seem unimportant that a miserable person is forced to confess to a crime. But in the sweep of history, a nation that accepts that practice as normal, a country that engages in wire-tapping, a people that exalts the ends over the means have no claim to a position of moral leadership among the nations.

I submit that my case cannot fairly be judged if it is not considered in its full context and in all its implications.

Mr. President, I have completed my presentation.

I do not ask for mercy.

I ask for justice. . . .

MR. BROOKE. Mr. President, I have listened very attentively to the debate. It appears that the two charges against Senator Dodd are very clear. One involves double billing. It would appear that in arriving at our decision, we should be looking for whether the Senator inadvertently or by negligence double billed. There is no question that there has been double billing, as I understand it. The Senator has admitted there was double billing. But we would want to know whether there had been negligence in the double billing, or inadvertence in the double billing, or whether there was any intention on the part of the Senator from Connecticut to double bill. Did he direct that there be double billing; or did some of his employees double bill without his knowledge?

These are the questions that we must resolve.

On the second charge, the charge of the misuse of funds, it is important to note that at no time during his presentation did Senator Dodd direct himself to the question of whether the money was used for political or personal purposes. I presumed, therefore, that Senator Dodd had not gotten past the first question, and he assumed the moneys had been contributed to be used for personal purposes. Therefore, he did not get into such questions as income taxes or repairs upon his home.

Reasonable men could not disagree that these would be personal matters. Obviously, income tax money or money used for the repair of a person's home is personal usage of money.

I take it Senator Dodd has not denied it. I, therefore, assume that Senator Dodd's position, so far as the personal use of funds is concerned, is based upon his contention that they were contributed to him to be used as he saw fit, and not purely for political purposes. . . .

The question still comes back to: What was in the minds of the persons who contributed to any or all of these dinners? Did they contribute their money to be used for political purposes, or did they contribute their money to Senator Dodd to use as he saw fit?

If we arrive at that decision, and we find the money was contributed solely for political purposes, then we do not have to go further, because Senator Dodd has already admitted he used that money for personal purposes. . . .

MR. GORE. I would disagree with the able Senator from Massachusetts that the purposes for which the funds were contributed are the key here. The key is the use of the office for the solicitation, for the obtaining of the funds used for personal purposes.

The Senator from Connecticut says this was intended by the contributors, and I take it intended by himself. So the question here really is, it seems to me, one of what is propriety.

MR. COOPER. Mr. President, will the Senator yield?

MR. GORE. If the Senator will permit me to finish——

MR. BROOKE. May I ask just one question? Is the Senator

saying it is improper for a U.S. Senator to receive a gift of money under any circumstances?

Mr. Gore. I am not saying that. . . .

Mr. Cooper. Will the Senator yield so that I may respond to the Senator from Tennessee?

Mr. Brooke. Yes.

Mr. Cooper. I believe that the Senator from Tennessee has arrived at the very crux of the question. If a Senator collected funds for himself under the guise that they were collected for campaign purposes, or if he collected campaign funds and appropriated them to his use, I think we would all have to agree that it would be improper.

But the committee did go farther, and that is shown by the language of its recommendation, at least in my view. We said that to use the office of a Senator to collect funds for his use for personal benefit through testimonials is improper.

I thank the Senator.

Mr. Brooke. Is that what the committee is basing its charge upon, that the use of the office to collect funds for your own personal use is improper?

Mr. Cooper. This is what the resolution says:

> Resolved, That it is the judgment of the Senate that the Senator from Connecticut, Thomas J. Dodd, for having engaged in a course of conduct over a period of five years from 1961 to 1965 of exercising the influence and power of his office as a United States Senator, as shown by the conclusions in the Investigation by the Select Committee on Standards and Conduct,
> (a) to obtain, and use for his personal benefit—

Mr. Brooke. But the resolution has to be read in its entirety— . . .

It says:

> (a) to obtain, and use for his personal benefit, funds from the public through political testimonials and a political campaign, and
> (b) to request and accept reimbursements for expenses from both the Senate and private organizations for the same travel.

My point is that you cannot read the resolution without reading it in its entirety, and you cannot divorce it.

In order for us to come to a conclusion, and to pass favorably upon the resolution, we have to find, one, that the Senator received moneys from the public through political testimonials, and used them for his personal benefit; or two, requested and accepted reimbursements for expenses from both the Senate and private organizations for the same travel.

We are not here called upon just to censure the Senator from Connecticut because of impropriety. We are called upon to censure him for some specific acts of wrongdoing that he has committed, and they are set forth in the resolution. I do not see how we can say we are simply called upon to censure him because of impropriety. . . .

MR. CASE. I wish to further sharpen the issue by this inquiry. Let us suppose you were approached by the committee and quite well understood the proceeds of this dinner might be used for Senator Dodd's personal obligations, for his personal benefit, and not part of his political expenses.

In view of the other factors, that is to say, that this was a part of a repeated series of dinners over a number of years, having in mind that he is a Senator of the United States, that this dinner was given to him, not just as Tom Dodd, the fellow down the street, but Tom Dodd, U.S. Senator, would this still, in your judgment, be not that sort of impropriety which would justify a resolution of censure by the Senate? You knew this was intended to raise money for his personal expense, and suppose everybody else felt the same way about it.

If someone came to me and asked me to make a contribution for a dinner to be given to Senator Dodd, and I was told at the time that the purpose of the fundraising event was to raise funds for Senator Dodd's personal use, your question is, "Do you think that that would be an impropriety on his part?"

If it is put in the context of being a part of a course of conduct over a number of years, in which a number of events of this sort had occurred, and a total of perhaps half a million dollars was raised——

MR. BROOKE. I do not know that. The Senator is adding a great many factors.

MR. CASE. I am adding only what I understand to be, roughly, the factual background as a part of the context.

MR. BROOKE. But are not those conclusions? Are not those the very things we are trying to find out? Are we not trying to determine whether they actually happened?

. . . It seems to me that the Senator from New Jersey is going back to the question raised by the distinguished senior Senator from Oregon [Mr. Morse] as to whether it is an impropriety for a U.S. Senator to have testimonial dinners, the income from which is to be for his personal use. This all very well may be wrong. But the United States Senate, to the best of my knowledge, at no time has ever said it is wrong, and there are no rules or guidelines by which a U.S. Senator can be bound. So far as that is concerned, and as I responded to the distinguished Senator from Oregon, this is a matter of a man's own, individual conscience and decision. I do not think that in this case we can apply such a rule, because there are no such rules that we can work by.

We get, then, into an ex post facto part of the case: whether there are such rules that we can use to govern this case. I know of no such rules, unless the Senator from New Jersey can cite them. . . .

MR. TOWER. The Senator has raised a fundamental question. If we are operating under due process of law and consonant with all its safeguards, the burden of proof falls on the accuser. If we are operating consonant with due process, it occurs to me there can be no due process unless there is a code, a law, a statute, something to which we can repair.

The Senate has been in existence almost 200 years, and our failure to adopt any code or standards of conduct must be construed as an intent not to do so. Then, by what standards do we judge a Senator?

I personally do not believe it is proper for a U.S. Senator to solicit funds publicly for private purposes. I disapprove of what the Senator from Connecticut did, if indeed he did it; but that does not mean we should give our efforts to deciding an issue involving a Senator by flying in the teeth of the Anglo-Saxon theory of the law.

If there is no code in existence, how can we condemn a man? If there is no code in existence, there is no precedent. . . .

MR. MOSS. Mr. President, I will vote to censure my personal friend, Senator Thomas J. Dodd. This decision has been made in anguish and in sorrow. In most of its aspects, the career of

Senator Dodd is a distinguished one. It is impossible not to sympathize with a prominent public figure who finds himself in such a position, and particularly to regret the trial that has been borne—and will be borne—by his family.

If I were voting for myself alone, I would be compassionate—I would forgive this fellow man. Tom Dodd has already paid a heavy price. He has been debased, humiliated, shamed, his good name tarnished. Were I to vote against censure, it would, in part, relieve the heavy burden which presses against my heart.

But my vote must speak not only for my conscience, but for my people in Utah, and for all of the people of the United States. I must vote as a representative of millions of Americans. The stark fact is that the national implications of this case place it far beyond consideration of its effect on one man, or on one man's family, unfortunate as that may be.

Senator Dodd, to his credit, requested the Select Committee on Ethics and Conduct to undertake its investigation. The committee members devoted many hours to hearings and to consideration of the evidence. The investigation has been thorough. It has been carefully conducted in a judicious manner. The committee's report, and the recommendations made therein, are entitled to great weight. My decision to vote to support the committee's recommendation was made after studying its report and the statements of Senator Dodd relating to it, and listening to many hours of debate on this Senate floor. Like my fellow Senators I have given most careful attention to the record and the debate and I have pondered long.

An ugly aspect of this case is the theft from Senator Dodd's office of thousands of personal letters and other documents. I commend the select committee for condemning these disloyal acts, and I join in such condemnation. My indignation towers at such perfidy.

The Senate's action in the matter before us will serve too little purpose if it results only in the censure of one Senator. A motion to censure is before us, but the Senate itself is on trial. Saying this, I emphatically do not imply that the ethical standards of the Congress are declining. In my opinion, the reverse is true. Further, Senators' conduct compares favorably with that of elected officials throughout the Nation. Nevertheless, the Congress faces a crisis of confidence.

Millions of Americans believe that many congressional Members are guilty of unethical practices. While Senator Dodd must bear the responsibility for his own acts, all of us are partially responsible for this public attitude. The Congress itself is on trial because we have failed to formulate and adopt concrete rules or codes of ethics to govern the conduct of Members.

It is true that many in the Nation exaggerate the facts. It is true that the issues are tried in the newspapers even before investigations are begun. And allegations of wrongdoing are sledgehammered home with numbing repetition and damning innuendo. But this, too, is partly our fault—we have permitted the sore to fester so long that human reaction is to believe every accusation that is hurled.

What is called for now? What must be done to restore the confidence of the Nation in its Congress? . . .

It is unfortunate that the case before us was preceded by two others which generated tremendous publicity on the question of congressional ethics—those of Bobby Baker and Representative Adam Clayton Powell. These three cases have brought the character of every Member of Congress into question.

Further, and much more important, the integrity of our Government itself has been brought into question. Under the division of power, it is the legislative branch which most directly represents the States and the people. If our integrity is questioned, the foundations of self-government are threatened. Our mail from constituents, as well as the opinion of the press and broadcasting media, indicate widespread dissatisfaction with: First, campaign financing; second, undue influence being exerted on Members; and third, expenses and emoluments of office. To these we must address ourselves.

The task of the Select Committee on Ethics and of the Senate has been a particularly difficult one because it has been necessary to combine to some degree the functions of lawgiver, prosecutor, judge, and jury—functions which under our legal concepts should be separate. First, Senators have had to examine the facts. Then we have had to decide whether those facts have brought disrepute on the Senate—and to decide what "disrepute" amounts to.

How much fairer it would be if there existed a clearly stated code against which the actions of any Senator could be judged.

We are accustomed to issues which have been raised or aggravated by the rapid changes taking place in our society. To some extent, the questions I have been discussing fall into this class. Whatever rules of conduct may have been adequate for the Senate of Webster and Calhoun, of LaFollette or Norris or Taft, those now in use will not do for the 1960's. In our own interest as Senators and in the interest of the great Federal Union which we serve, we must regulate more adequately both conduct in office and campaign financing.

It is my sincere hope that this unhappy occasion will be an impetus to correction of the evils of which it is a symptom, and that we may look forward to the timely enactment of firm correctives.

With a very heavy heart will I vote for censure. In fierce political conflicts, where victories are narrow and the results are of overriding consequence to the course of wise and enlightened government, it is so easy to rationalize that the end justifies the means. Those of us who are elected begin to feel a proprietary right to our positions, and justify ourselves.

God help me to remember the bitter lesson of today. . . .

[*By a narrow margin, the Senate voted to strike the charge of double-billing, but then voted censure based on the other charge 92–5, three senators being absent because of illness. Those voting against censure included: Senator Russell B. Long of Louisiana, who was Dodd's principal defender in the debate; senators Thurmond and Tower, Republicans; Senator Ribicoff, Dodd's colleague from Connecticut, and Senator Dodd himself.*]

MR. STENNIS. . . . I feel that the adoption of this resolution, in a way, is a new start for the Senate. I hope it is a new start for Senator Dodd. I say further, with emphasis, that all of us had a great deal of personal sympathy for him from the very beginning. He has behaved, it seemed to me, under all this pressure, in a very exemplary way.

There is no other point that I can make, there is no criticism of any Senator, no victory here for anyone, and no victory against anyone. I think the Senate realized it had to face this matter, and it did, in great measure; and I believe that means a constructive new start. . . .

MR. MANSFIELD. Mr. President, the past 2 weeks have been difficult—even painful—for all Members of the Senate. But our situation can in no way compare with that of the distinguished Senator from Connecticut [Mr. Dodd]. Compelled to sit in judgment, the Senate has met and discharged its responsibility.

But of significant note during these past days has been the manner, the conduct, and the courage of our colleague from Connecticut.

In rendering its judgment, the Senate has been attentive to the substance and gravity of the issue just decided. But it has also witnessed a man under extreme pressure and strain whose response to the adversity was such that each Senator may henceforth—in good conscience and in all sincerity—refer to the Senator from Connecticut as his friend and colleague.

Reform and the Future of the Senate

The two essays which conclude this volume are presented as parts of a debate, yet they were not written so. Their titles have been supplied editorially. Senator Clark was addressing himself directly to the question of Congressional reform, but Senator Ervin was not. Rather, he was attempting to define the role that the Senate can and should, in his view, fulfill in the American political system.

It is significant, however, that the two are in agreement about the issues involved on both counts. Senator Clark cannot confine himself to the Senate, or even to Congress alone. To achieve the reform he desires he must ge beyond them to other elements, particularly the party system. Senator Ervin, on the other side, sees the impact of the larger system on the Senate, and stresses the indeterminacy of the decisions made in the American party and electoral processes. For him, the fact that policy choices are not clearly made in elections leaves it to the Senate and to the Congress generally to re-think and to scrutinise with care any questions on which controversy still lingers. Thus, by accepting the party system as it is, he must defend the legislative procedures to which it is linked.

Together, these essays constitute a debate about the present and the future of the political system as a whole, and the part that the legislative branch—the Senate especially—should play in it.

XIV. The Case for Congressional Reform

Senator Joseph S. Clark

ON MAY 10, 1965, THE CONGRESS OF THE UNITED STATES began the first major examination of its organization and operation in twenty years, when the Joint Committee on the Organization of the Congress, under the Co-Chairmanship of Senator A. S. Mike Monroney and Representative Ray J. Madden, opened its hearings in the Old Supreme Court Chamber in the Capitol.

Only once before in our history had such a study been conducted. The first Joint Committee on the Organization of the Congress was formed in 1945 under the Co-Chairmanship of Senator Robert M. LaFollette, Jr. and then Representative A. S. Mike Monroney. Its work culminated in the adoption of the Legislative Reorganization Act of 1946.

Many valuable reforms were incorporated in that act. Among other things, it greatly reduced the number of standing committees in both houses, abolished certain overlaps in committee jurisdiction, and gave Members of Congress more adequate staff assistance.

But many more badly needed reforms were not enacted, partly because a sufficient consensus could not be developed in support of some of the Joint Committee's recommendations, but more importantly because the Joint Committee was specifically prohibited from making recommendations for reforming the rules, parliamentary procedure, practices and/or precedents of either house.

To even the casual student of Congress it should be evident that such a limitation was bound to be self-defeating. The major source of the problem—in fact the principal seat of the Congress' malady—lies precisely within the prohibited area: the rules, parliamentary procedures, practices and/or precedents of either house.

When the same limiting language was placed in the resolution creating the Monroney-Madden committee I fought, unfortunately in vain, to have it stricken. It was, and continues to be my view that trying to reform the Congress without revising and modernizing its rules and procedures is like trying to cure a patient ill of appendicitis without operating. It cannot be done.

That view, in my opinion, is fully borne out by the Legislative Reorganization Act of 1967, which passed the Senate on March 7, 1967 (and now languishes in the House), and was largely the result of the efforts of that committee working under the handicaps imposed on it. The Act contains a number of reforms, and for that reason I supported it. But it would be wrong to believe that it will amount to meaningful congressional reform even if finally enacted, because it does not.

The time has not yet come, and it may not be just around the corner, when a comprehensive reform of the rules, procedures, customs, and practices of the Congress, and of the Senate especially, will take place. Yet I believe that it is in sight. It must come if the Congress is to survive as a coequal partner in our three-branch Federal Government. A long-range, world-wide, historic trend has witnessed the progressive gravitation of governmental power from legislative into executive branches; a peculiarly American development of this trend has resulted in increasing the negative power of the Congress while impairing its power to act positively in solving the complex and vexing problems of our time. The power to say "no" or indeed to make no reply at all has been enhanced. Costly weakening and sometimes unfortunate compromise for badly needed legislation is the inevitable result of the system under which we operate. We are legislating in an archaic manner, and the times demand change in order to keep up with the pace of the 20th century—and the last third of the 20th century at that. For change is the essence of the world—change and growth—and institutions that cannot change and grow to meet the demands of the world are condemned to shatter under pressures they cannot contain, and be cast aside.

What I propose to do in this paper is to discuss the changes which must be made to convert the Congress into an effective instrument capable of translating majority will into enacted legislation in a reasonably prompt fashion.

Under the major heading of internal reforms I shall treat three subheadings: first, reforms affecting the rules, precedents, practices, and procedures of the Congress with a primary emphasis on the Senate; second, reforms affecting the party structure and organization within the Congress; and third, reforms having to do with problems of conflict of interest within the legislative branch.

Under the major heading of external reforms I shall deal with such subjects as campaign finances, terms of office of Representatives and Senators, and other matters.

INTERNAL REFORMS

A. *Rules, Precedents, Practices, and Procedures.*

Shortly after I was first elected to the United States Senate as a Democrat from Pennsylvania in November 1956, I got some advice and counsel on how to conduct myself in the Senate from an old friend who now happens to be the Vice President of the United States. The sum and substance of what he said was this: "Keep your mouth shut and your eyes open. The Senate is a friendly, courteous place. You will clash on the filibuster rule with Dick Russell and the Southerners as soon as you take your oath of office. But don't let your ideology embitter your personal relationships."

After a series of clashes, in 1957 and again in 1959, it became apparent to me that the fundamental problem with the Senate was that it lacked the capacity to act when a majority was ready for action, and that although the filibuster was the principal weapon of obstruction, it was far from being the only one.

Having concluded that basic changes in the organization of the Senate were required, on July 1, 1960 I offered a series of resolutions to amend the Senate rules, arguing that:

> The great difficulty which the Congress is having in passing needed legislation before adjournment calls attention once again to the

archaic and undemocratic rules and procedures under which we on Capitol Hill attempt to legislate.

The harsh fact is that the present rules and methods of operation of the Senate and of the House are stacked against the people of the United States. They penalize those who seek action in the national interest. They reward those who cling to an outmoded status quo which threatens our very survival.

... In my judgment, there is no other legislative body in the free world as incapable of action, when action is desired by a large majority but strongly resisted by a minority, as the Senate of the United States.

Nothing happened with the rules changes which I introduced in 1960, nor did I expect that anything would. They languished in the Senate Rules Committee, to which they had been referred, and expired at the end of the 86th Congress. They met the same fate when I reintroduced them in the 87th Congress, in the 88th Congress, and again in the 89th Congress. The only noticeable forward motion occurred when, in the 88th Congress, watered-down versions of proposals I had made dealing with germaneness of debate, and permission for committees to sit while the Senate is in session were adopted, and in the 90th Congress, when an enlarged permission for committees to sit during sessions, provisions for proxy voting on committees, and a committee bill of rights were incorporated into the Legislative Reorganization Act. If that Act passes the House, which at this writing appears doubtful, it will constitute more progress than has been achieved in all the years of my service.

Meanwhile, the job of refining, perfecting, and elaborating the proposed rules changes has been progressing. As a result of this work, after more than half a year of effort on the part of the Legislative Reference Service of the Library of Congress and my staff, operating under my direction, a comprehensive revision of the entire Standing Rules of the Senate was completed. So far as I know, this is the first attempt at a top-to-bottom rewrite of the Rules of the Senate since the days of Thomas Jefferson. It was first introduced by me at the close of the 88th Congress. I reintroduced it in the 89th Congress and again in the 90th Congress.

Unfortunately it is not practical for me to discuss here all of the important changes contained in this comprehensive revision of the

Senate Rules, but I would like to mention a few of the most significant ones.*

Because the filibuster is the principal enemy of majority rule, let me turn first to my proposal for an anti-filibuster rule:

1. *Motion for the Previous Question.* Actually, there is nothing new about this procedure, since it originated in Jefferson's Manual, was in effect in the Senate until 1809, and is in use today in the House of Representatives and in virtually every other legislative body in the civilized world. My proposal does however include some modifications to protect Senatorial sensibilities and guarantee a reasonable period for debate.

Under this new rule the cumbersome and unwieldly cloture provisions of Rule XXII would be deleted and in their place would be substituted a split-level motion, by which a majority of Senators present and voting could terminate debate: (1) on any motion or amendment to a measure pending before the Senate after that motion or amendment had received 15 hours of consideration on not less than 3 calendar days; or (2) on the principal measure itself, together with any motions or amendments relating to it, after the measure plus all related motions and amendments had received consideration for 15 calendar days.

If the motion passes by a majority vote, 1 hour of debate equally divided between opponents and proponents would be allowed on any motion or amendment encompassed by the motion, and 4 hours, divided in the same manner, would be allowed on final passage.

Not only would this do away with the situation which presently exists, where 34 determined Senators can prevent action indefinitely against the will of the other 66—it would also permit expeditious action once debate had been terminated. The present rule allows for an additional hour of debate—by every Senator who wishes to speak—and that can be a very long and weary time, particularly since the clock stops while votes on amendments are being recorded. During the consideration of the Civil Rights Act of 1964, Senator Thurmond of South Carolina was able to call for

* For the rest, see the *Congressional Record* of September 23, 1964, which contains a side-by-side comparative print of the present rules and my proposals, and an explanatory memorandum.

record votes on 23 amendments proposed by him during the one hour of debate alloted to him after cloture. He held the floor for a whole day by this procedure.

A second major problem arises because of the tendency of certain bills to get "pickled" in certain committees. The classic case is the Senate Judiciary Committee, which has come to be called the "graveyard of civil rights legislation." It was because of this reputation that the Civil Rights Act of 1964 was not referred to committee in the Senate at all, but was intercepted on the floor before referral to committee after it had been passed by the House. For the same reason the Voting Rights Act of 1965 was sent to the Judiciary Committee subject to a unanimous consent agreement which required the committee to report the bill back to the Senate on a date certain. It was feared, and with good reason, that without such an order the bill would never have emerged from the committee.

The technique I have recommended for dealing with this problem is:

2. *Motion to instruct a committee to report on a major legislative matter.* Although it is axiomatic that the committees of the Senate are its creatures and agents, no effective procedures presently exist by which the Senate can exercise its authority in a fair, orderly, and effective manner.

The rules do presently provide for a motion to discharge a committee from further consideration of a measure. But this motion cannot be used to secure committee consideration of a subject, nor does it provide a device for obtaining a committee's recommendations. Moreover, such a motion can be filibustered, since it is debatable.

This proposal remedies these defects by creating a privileged motion to denominate any measure pending in committee or subcommittee as a "major legislative matter." This motion would not be subject to filibuster, provided that a notice of intention to make such a motion had been presented on the previous calendar day, and printed in the *Congressional Record*.

Debate on the motion would be limited to 8 hours, the time to be divided equally between opponents and proponents. Such motion, if carried by a majority of Senators present and voting, would constitute an instruction to the committee in which the measure was then pending to report it to the Senate within 30 calendar days, by poll or otherwise, with the recommendation (a) that it be passed, or (b) that it not be passed, or (c) that it be passed with amendments, stating the recommended amendments.

3. *Selection and retirement of committee chairmen.* The surest guarantee that the majority will rule in committee is to ensure that the chairman of that committee is responsive to the majority will. Under my proposed rules changes, chairmen of the standing committees would be chosen by secret ballot of the majority members of the committee at the beginning of each new Congress. I have no doubt that nine times out of ten the result would be the same as obtained now under the seniority rule—the majority member with the most seniority on the committee would be chosen. But in the tenth case, a would-be chairman who was arbitrary or out-of-step with the majority members would be rejected, and this would serve as a useful warning to other chairmen to refrain from arbitrary or dictatorial conduct.

In addition, no Senator would be permitted to serve as chairman of a standing committee after he had attained the age of 70. It is true that in some cases the Senate would lose the services as chairman of a Senator still fully able to carry that great burden. But in far more cases the rule would serve the general good by vesting the responsibilities of chairmanship in a younger, more vigorous, and more capable man. This is the general experience in business and on the Courts.

4. *Germaneness of debate.* I can think of nothing more frustrating and more puzzling to the visitor in the Senate gallery than the irrational leaping from subject to subject which frequently characterizes what passes for debate on the Senate floor. And I know for certain of nothing more frustrating to the Senator charged with responsibility for floor managing a bill than to have the flow of debate interrupted, and final passage of the measure inexcusably delayed—to the inconvenience of virtually everyone—by a long and wholly irrelevant discourse on one Senator's pet concern.

The present rule, adopted in the 88th Congress, provides for only a three hour germaneness period every day. Once the three hour period is over, the protection of the rule is gone. The proposal in the comprehensive revision is far more flexible. It provides that a majority of the Senate, on a non-debatable motion, could require further debate on the pending business to be germane to the subject matter until the business is disposed of, whether it be 5 hours or 5 days.

5. *Germaneness of amendments.* The House rules presently provide that amendments must be germane to the subject matter of the provision being amended, but there is presently no such rule in the Senate. My proposal is similar to that in use in the House. Questions of germaneness would be decided by the Presiding Officer subject to appeal to the Senate without debate. The abuse of the present procedure in the Senate was evidenced when Senator Dirksen proposed a non-germane rider to an American Legion Baseball resolution which would have overruled Court decisions requiring the reapportionment of state legislatures on a one man, one vote basis.

6. *Three-hour rule.* One of the most lamentable aspects of the folklore of the Senate has to do with endurance contests for non-stop speeches in which Senators pit themselves against the record books to try to set new records for long-windedness. Such exhibitions make a mockery of a body which calls itself "deliberative." Under my proposal, whenever a Senator spoke for more than three consecutive hours, an objection that he take his seat could compel him to yield the floor.

7. *Committee bill of rights.* Another guarantee of democracy within the Senate's committees—which is where most of the work is done—would be the adoption of uniform and fair codes of procedure to govern committee operations. Some steps towards this are incorporated in the Legislative Reorganization Act of 1967 and will considerably enhance the position of committee members if that Act is adopted. Under my proposed committee "bill of rights," a majority of the members of each standing committee would be authorized, in addition to the procedures now provided in the individual committee rules, to convene meetings; to direct the initiation, conduct, and termination of hearings; to call up bills for consideration; and to terminate debate in committee after a measure has received committee consideration in executive session for a total of 5 hours.

8. *Limit on committee memberships.* One of the things that makes a Senator's life particularly difficult is that his multiple committee obligations often require him to be in two, possibly

three, and sometimes even in four different committee meetings at the same time. It is par for the course for me to have to shuttle back and forth between the Senate Foreign Relations Committee, which is a very busy committee with extremely heavy responsibilities, the Labor and Public Welfare Committee's Employment and Manpower Subcommittee, which I chair, and which has a heavy schedule of its own, and the Rules Committee where I am working to get the rules changes we are presently discussing adopted. The answer is to crack down on multiple committee assignments—to reduce the number of committees to which a Senator can belong, so as to permit him to do a decent job with each. In my view, no Senator should be permitted to serve on more than two committees. It is perfectly feasible, from a mathematical point of view, to reduce memberships in this way while permitting the committees to remain large enough to reflect accurately party ratios.

B. *Party Structure and Organization.*

Almost as important as the Senate Rules in the proper functioning of the Senate is the structure and organization of the two parties.

1. *Party Conferences.* In a series of brilliant speeches on the Senate floor, beginning in February 1959, Senator William Proxmire complained that "the Typical Democratic Senator has literally nothing to do with determining the legislative program and politics of his party." He protested the total disappearance of the party caucus as an instrument of decision or even information. He concocted an epitaph:

> Here lies the Democratic caucus
> Conceived by Senatorial responsibility
> And born with the Democratic Party—1800,
> Assassinated at the hand of Senatorial indifference—1953.
> She labored faithfully and well to make
> Senatorial leadership responsible to all the people.

Although some progress has been made since Senator Proxmire spoke, much remains to be done. There should be regular meeting days for the Democratic Conference to formalize what is now a hit-or-miss performance. The initial object of these meetings should be to determine in general terms the legislative program for the coming session, based on the State of the Union, Budget and Economic messages of the President, and reported by the Democratic members of the Joint Economic Committee. The recommendations of the Policy Committee and of the leadership on these matters would naturally carry great weight with the conference.

Such formal action by the conference, based on written reports and a written agenda circulated in advance, would act as a curb on the tendency of the legislative committees to go their own way without much regard for party position or authority. What Woodrow Wilson said in 1885 is equally true today:

> [The caucus is a vital] antidote to the committees, designed to supply the cohesive principle which the multiplicity and mutual independence of the committees so powerfully tend to destroy. The caucus is the drilling ground of the party. There its discipline is renewed and strengthened, its uniformity of step and gesture regained.

2. *Steering Committee.* In order to assure that the composition of the legislative committees appropriately reflects the ideological composition of the Senate as a whole, it is essential that certain reforms of the Democratic Steering Committee—which serves as the Democratic committee on committees in the Senate—be carried out.

The Steering Committee, recently expanded by the addition of two new members, now numbers 17—including the Majority Leader, the Whip, and the Secretary of the Democratic Conference, all of whom serve ex officio with full voting privileges.

The requisites for a Steering Committee dedicated to democracy within the Senate democratic membership are: (1) that it should serve for only two years, the duration of a single Congress; (2) that its members, other than the leadership, should not be eligible for re-election until two years after their initial terms have expired; (3) that members should be nominated by the leader, seeking such advice as he thinks desirable; (4) that they should be subject to confirmation or rejection by the conference, which should have the right by majority vote taken by secret ballot to make substitutions to the list submitted by the Majority Leader; and (5) that the non-leadership members thus selected should represent a fair cross section of the geographical and ideological representation of the party in the Senate.

Once such a Steering Committee is appointed and functioning it could be trusted (1) to fill committee vacancies with the best interests of the party and the program in mind and (2) to recommend to the Conference such disciplinary measures in terms of committee selection and seniority against recalcitrants as disagreeable necessity might require.

There is no serious problem on the Republican side of the Senate. Its conference now meets regularly and selects its committees for terms of two years on the basis of nominations by the chairman of the conference itself. The ideological and geographical representation on its Committee on Committees appears to meet the above recommendations. In short the Republican Senators democratized their conference a good many years ago.

3. *Policy Committee.* A thorough overhauling and rebuilding of the Policy Committees of both parties in both houses is also a necessity. The Democratic Policy Committee in the Senate should be a committee of seven on which the leadership should serve as full members constituting a majority of the committee, as recommended by the LaFollette-Monroney Committee in 1945. It is desirable to strengthen the leadership and make the size of the meetings with the House Committee and with the President and his White House advisers manageable. The three members in addition to the leadership should be nominated by the leadership subject to confirmation by the conference. *All three of these Senators should be wholeheartedly committed to the platform of the party and the program of the President.* Unlike the Steering Committee, geography should play no part in this selection. The test of membership should be party loyalty and prestige in the Senate. While seniority would undoubtedly have a bearing on the choice, it should not be the determining factor.

The function of the Senate Policy Committee would be to work with the House Policy Committee and the President on the tactics and strategy of enacting the party platform into law.

Since continuity of policy is important and since the prestige of the Policy Committee should be sufficient to bring the chairmen of the Legislative Committees into line behind the program, it would seem wiser to make membership on the committee indefinite in term, i.e., the members to serve like federal judges for as long as they behave themselves in office. Stated somewhat differently, they should serve at the pleasure of the conference, which, as in the case of the leadership, would probably mean until death, defeat, resignation, or repudiation.

Since the leadership would be in the majority, such a Policy Committee could be trusted not to abuse the "traffic cop" functions now exercised by the present committee, and should be given this power.

The effect of these changes would be to strengthen greatly the Presidential party, to create an agency of high prestige with the mission of making party performance match party promise, and to give party responsibility the lift it needs in the Congress to make that institution's behavior more acceptable to the American people.

C. *Conflict of Interest.*

One effect of the Bobby Baker case has been to focus public attention on ethics in Congress. Having participated as a member of the Senate Rules Committee in the lengthy and exhaustive investigation into Baker's wheeling and dealing, I am more than ever convinced that the greatest need is for a compulsory system of comprehensive financial disclosure for Senate officers and employees, and for Senators as well.

Under my proposal, Senators and Senate staff members would be required to make public disclosure of such matters as assets, liabilities, capital gains, and items of non-official income (including gifts and expense payments) in excess of $100. Interests could not be covered up by using the name of a straw man or a spouse. In addition, connections with firms and financial enterprises would have to be made public. Relations with lobbyists, and moonlighting by staff persons would also come under regulation.

EXTERNAL REFORMS

Acceptance of the reforms I have proposed would go a long way toward making it possible for the Congress to act responsibly when a majority in the Congress is ready to act. These reforms are, of course, institutional; they are internal.

There remains, however, the problem of assuring that the Congress truly represents the majority will of the American people as expressed in national elections. There is reason to believe that today it does not. And it is very important that it should, primarily because the success of our reform of the Congress is to some extent dependent on the proper working of our political processes.

The relationship between the political system and the organization, rules, customs, and procedures of Congress is reciprocal. A change in one will very likely in the long run produce changes in the other. Just as the performance of the modern President reflects the composition of the Electoral College, so today's Congressional performance reflects the process by which its members are elected.

A. *Campaign Finances*

The subject of money in politics has received much deserved attention in recent years. There is general agreement that some method must be found for securing mass financial support for political candidates. The pernicious consequences of reliance on a few wealthy contributors for large donations is obvious.

The recent enactment and later suspension by the Congress of Senator Russell Long's plan for direct federal payments to defray campaign expenses of Presidential candidates is evidence of this concern. This approach may well raise as many problems as it solves, and in any event will require a good deal of careful study.

My preference has been for the approach recommended by the Heard Commission on Campaign Costs, appointed by President Kennedy in 1961. That approach relied primarily on tax incentives for individual contributions.

These recommendations, if implemented, would go far toward transferring the support of politics to the ordinary citizen, without involving resort to a government subsidy determined by a cumbersome and arbitrary formula. They might well eliminate the need for larger contributions.

Perhaps even more important than the technical means of achieving mass financial support for the parties is the Commission's recommendation that the money be disbursed through the

National Committees and state committees designated by them. Obviously this would place a disciplinary weapon of the first importance in the hands of the national party agencies. It would create a powerful centralizing force in American politics to counter the decentralizing forces present elsewhere. It would substitute national for parochial direction of the parties' financial efforts and concerns.

None of this can be done without a heightened concern for policy, particularly national policy, on the part of the parties. People will contribute their money voluntarily to a cause, as the results of thousands of volunteer civic and welfare organizations attest. But except for those who seek jobs or favors they are not entitled to, or who are "maced" by unscrupulous political leaders and hold jobs without Civil Service protection, they will not willingly contribute in order to maintain an amoral political machine in power.

B. *Registration and Voting Reforms*

In adopting the Voting Rights Act of 1965, Congress dealt with the most pressing problem connected with registration and voting—the deprivation of the Negro's constitutional right to vote as a result of systematic discrimination in certain areas of the South. Other problems, however, still require our attention. It is a serious commentary on the health of our institutions that a century and three-quarters after the adoption of the Constitution we have not yet achieved a national definition of the right to vote nor a country-wide determination to protect the exercise of this right.

Millions of Americans in competitive election districts are prevented from voting by absurdly high residence requirements, prohibitions against absentee voting, or cumbersome registration procedures that erect unnecessary obstacles. All these barriers may have at one time been genuinely designed to eliminate fraud. They combine now to discriminate seriously against an increasingly mobile population without achieving much in the way of electoral honesty. Some eight million adult Americans did not vote in the last Presidential election, for example, because they could not meet state and local residence requirements. These cumbersome and antiquated obstacles to full voting participation can and must be removed. To this end, it is encouraging to note that the Johnson Administration recently submitted to the Congress a bill which would eliminate antiquated residence requirements and greatly facilitate absentee voting.

C. *Constitutional Amendments to eliminate off-year elections for Senators and Representatives*

The forces of nationalism as opposed to parochialism, the forces of democracy as opposed to oligarchy and plutocracy, and the ability of the President to obtain enactment of the platform on which he ran and was elected would all be strengthened if elections to both the House and Senate were held only in Presidential years. This could be accomplished by a constitutional amendment increasing the terms of Representatives to four years, decreasing the terms of Senators to four years, and eliminating mid-term Congressional elections, thus calling for the election of the entire Senate at the time of each Presidential election, or, in the alternative, extending Senate terms to eight years with half elected at each Presidential election.

With regard to the House of Representatives, two years is too short a term in which to represent effectively a Congressional district. A newly-elected Congressman has hardly warmed his seat before he must leave it to campaign for renomination and reelection. And if he comes from a non-competitive district, he will remain a Representative for the rest of his political life. So what does it matter if he goes through the motions of getting reelected once every four years instead of once every two?

If he comes from a competitive district, he will be more of a statesman and less of an errand boy if he runs always at the same time and on the same ticket as the Presidential candidate of his party. The strengthening of the national interest in terms of the effective dialogue on issues which such a procedural change would bring about is substantial. The strengthening of the national parties is even more so. The strengthening of the hand of the President, who alone speaks for all Americans, is the most substantial of all.

Much the same thing can be said about the Senate. If our terms were cut to four years and we were forced to run in the same election as that in which the President was elected, we might make a useful contribution in our respective states to a quadrennial national debate on national issues and, if we backed the winning candidate, return to the Capitol prepared not to sabotage his program but to help him to enact it into law.

D. *Elimination of Political Patronage*

One political reform that needs to be extended is the elimination of political patronage at all levels of government.

The whole logic of the patronage process is to strengthen the worst local elements in the political system. A mayor's appointive power is vested in a ward leader, a governor's appointive power is delegated to a county leader, a President's power is exercised by a Senator or a Representative. The executive is held responsible for the appointee's performance, but the effective power of appointment is vested in those who share none of this responsibility. The effect of this immunity from responsibility is heartless and inefficient government.

Strengthening the national parties and increasing their concern with public policy thus require continued reduction of the role of patronage in political life. A start could be made by eliminating Senatorial confirmation of postmasters, as proposed in the Legislative Reorganization Act of 1967. Politicians cling to such powers with stubborn tenacity in spite of repeated demonstrations that patronage is no longer serviceable as a political weapon. More enemies than friends are made through political appointments unrelated to merit. Successful political careers are today increasingly built upon the exploitation of issues. The patronage-bloated political organization is contributing less and less to electoral victory as the level of voter education and sophistication rises. Nor is patronage necessary for the health of strong political parties. It serves only to strengthen elements in the political structure which are alien to the spirit of the age, hostile to the strengthening of the policy-oriented elements in the parties, and contrary to the dynamics of a healthy and competitive political system. And so, in the end, Congressional patronage makes for a less effective Congress.

CONCLUSION

This discussion of the needed reforms, both internal and external, has plainly been far from complete. Extremely important subjects such as the impact of legislative re-apportionment, the need for the creation of national party councils, and the ombudsman idea, which has been advanced by Congressman Henry Reuss and Senator Claiborne Pell, have not even been touched upon. But if, in this brief review, I have done no more than whet appetites and direct attention to the issues, that will be sufficient.

For never before in the history of this republic has there been so great a need to bring brainpower to the aid of government. The amazing legislative output of recent Congresses is a tribute to the unprecedented political gifts of President Johnson and the huge Democratic majorities of the Johnson landslide—but it is hardly evidence of any basic change in the Congressional structure and organization which deadlocked our democracy in 1963. It seems perfectly clear to me that when President Johnson vacates the White House, and perhaps even before then, and the party ratio becomes less lopsided, Congress will be its cranky, obstreperous, obstructionist self again.

That is why the initiative must be seized now. An enlightened public opinion and an Administration prepared to use its power and influence to effect the institutional changes needed to infuse life into the Congress can succeed. In that success lies the sole hope of the Congress for a return to the strength and vigor of a live and vital branch on our tripartite tree of government.

XV. The Case against Reform: A Nobler Purpose Than Political Efficiency

Senator Sam J. Ervin, Jr.

WE HEAR A GREAT DEAL TODAY ABOUT THE NEED FOR EFFIciency in government, particularly in the legislative branch of our government. Some Senators and Representatives persistently and sternly rebuke Congress for its cumbersome methods and procedures, political scientists read us learned lectures about it, and columnists, editorial writers, and magazine pundits inundate us in a flood of books and articles on the subject.

Because American efficiency has produced such spectacular results in agriculture and industry, we tend to welcome appeals of this kind with unquestioning gullibility. But efficiency is by no means the be-all and end-all of democratic government. That government is not necessarily best that is most efficient. Avoidable waste in government is certainly deplorable and ought constantly to be attacked, but democratic government has other values and nobler purposes. If the American historical experience has any meaning it is this: government is best when it is most representative and when it glorifies and gives maximum rein to liberty. We tolerate a certain amount of inefficiency because we know it is the price we must pay for liberty, and liberty is our highest priority.

When applied to our Federal legislature, and especially to the Senate, the doctrine of efficiency first and efficiency above all is generally accompanied by three particularly pernicious demands. First, we are instructed to give the Chief Executive our undevia-

THE CASE AGAINST REFORM

ting cooperation and acquiescence in all things. Second, we are told that good government can only result from acceptance of "party responsibility." Third, we are informed that the will of the "majority" must rule supreme.

Congress must obey the President, it is said, because he represents all the people rather than a segment of them, because he is capable of ruling firmly and decisively whereas Congress is not, and because only presidential rule can save us in an era of continuing crises. The text is taken from historian James MacGregor Burns who once wrote that:

> Under the conditions of crisis government in America, the sharing of power by President and Congress means the sapping of national authority in an era when our federal government must be strong enough to meet emergencies at home and abroad. . . . To force the President to share power equally with Congress would be to stunt the very agency that has supplied leadership and vision.*

I maintain that if Congress is not to share power with the Executive Branch, our liberties are lost. Congress as an institution represents all of the people as surely as does the President, and in some ways represents them more fully.

Presidents may rule firmly; then again, depending upon personality and ideology, they may not. As for our era of crises, all of American history is one long crisis. There is no more justification for one-man rule now than there was when the founding fathers gathered in Philadelphia to write the Constitution.

Those founding fathers profoundly understood the most grievous weakness of the argument for supreme presidential power. They had studied the history of mankind and pondered the long and unending battle for the right of self-government, for the right to be free from governmental tyranny. Their own experience and the bloody pages of history had taught them the sad but inescapable truth that government itself might be the deadliest foe to freedom. They had learned the lesson, reiterated more than a century later by Woodrow Wilson, that liberties never come from government but from the subjects of it. They believed with James Madison that if you concentrate all the powers of government in one man or one body of men you have established a tyranny, and

---

* *Congress On Trial,* p. 181.

it makes no difference whether you call it a monarchy or a republic, it is still a tyranny.

The founding fathers recognized that by its very nature government thirsts for power, that the thirst is insatiable, and that government will destroy freedom unless it is restrained from so doing by some law which it can neither nullify nor amend. They did not deny the necessity of government. What they denied was the necessity for absolute government, and the device they gave us to thwart absolutism was that of divided powers, of checks and balances. They divided power between the Federal Government on the one hand and the States on the other. Within the Federal Government, powers were distributed among the President, the Congress, and the judiciary. These were and remain the fundamental protections of our freedoms.

Such a system may indeed involve some inefficiency, and sometimes a great deal of it. Insofar as the legislative process is concerned, it is a system of successive cautious steps, of successive checks and rechecks, and of continuous accommodation and compromise. It is not streamlined; it was never meant to be. But it has this great and overriding virtue; it tends to check tyranny.

In my view, therefore, it is essential that Congress maintain its independence. A Senator should vote with a President when he believes that President's program is good for the country and not merely because it is the President who asks for it.

"Party responsibility" is one of those fascinating euphemisms which, when examined carefully, flows down a river of fallacious assumptions into an ocean of impractical, ridiculous, and dangerous conclusions. It boils down to this: A legislator ought to vote the way his party tells him to vote without concerning himself about his State, his country, or his conscience. W. S. Gilbert succinctly satirized that approach some 75 years ago:

> When in that House M.P.'s divide,
>   If they've a brain and cerebellum, too,
> They've got to leave that brain outside,
>   And vote just as their leaders tell 'em to.

In the name of party government and party unity, Members of Congress are ordered to follow the party line without question. Any deviation from that line arouses charges of party treason and demands that one leave or be expelled from the party.

THE CASE AGAINST REFORM

In the context of American political realities, this is absurd.

It is impractical because neither major party in this country is monolithic in thought or program. A few years ago one distinguished Senator suggested that no man be appointed chairman of a Senate committee unless his views on the subjects over which his committee has jurisdiction coincided with those of his party's platform. I replied that it is often impossible to determine what that platform means. Some provisions are put into party platforms to conceal rather than to reveal the party's position.

For example, in 1928 Al Smith, the Democratic candidate for the presidency, ran on a promise to repeal prohibition. For a long time the Republican candidate, Herbert Hoover, remained silent on this embarrassing question. When it became clear that he must say something about it, the Republican National Committee announced with great fanfare that the candidate was going to make his position crystal clear. And on the appointed day at the appointed time, Mr. Hoover said: "Prohibition is a noble experiment." Those who favored prohibition welcomed Hoover as a supporter; had he not said that prohibition was noble? And those who opposed prohibition argued that Hoover was on their side; had he not said it was an experiment, and was not an experiment something which was tried and failed? Which Republican chairmen of Senate committees were to be retained by their party, those who were for or those who opposed prohibition? And who was to make the decision?

I know something about the fashioning of party platforms, having served on the platform committee of the Democratic National Convention of 1960 in Los Angeles. We wrote and adopted a platform that, in substance, promised everyone in the United States whatever he wanted from the Federal treasury. That same platform also carried a plank promising to balance the budget. Obviously these planks were contradictory. If a Democratic Senator thereafter introduced a bill calling for the expenditure of enormous sums of Federal monies, and the chairman of the committee to which the bill was assigned opposed it, each could accuse the other of violating the party's platform, and with equal justification. The Senator introducing the bill could demand the chairman's removal because he was opposing one plank of the platform. The chairman could reply that passing such a bill would unbalance the budget and that therefore he, the chairman, more truly represented the platform. Who is to decide which man is carrying out the promises of the party?

Moreover, demands for stringent party regularity are ridiculous when applied to a group of legislators representing geographical areas that vary so widely in population and economic and social problems. The condition of both major parties illustrates the inevitable differences that must arise under these circumstances. Wisely, neither major party demands undeviating party regularity, for to do so would mean the party's disintegration.

John J. Parker, a distinguished jurist in my State, once remarked that, "The man who puts the welfare of his party above the welfare of his country is, in the last analysis, either a fool or a knave." He is a fool if he believes that any single party has a monopoly on political wisdom, that every single plank in his party's platform is sound. He is a knave if, knowing such positions are unsound and believing them to be detrimental to his country, he supports them for the sake of party advantage.

The lengths to which a fanatic apostle of unyielding party unity will go is no better illustrated than by Henry Wallace. Originally a Republican, he left that party because he could not get along with it, or it with him. Having joined the Democratic Party, he insisted upon party regularity and most especially on those measures he favored as Democratic Secretary of Agriculture. On one occasion, I heard him say that every Democrat who did not vote for the major pieces of legislation proposed by the Administration should be denied the right to sit on any congressional committee. Wallace's search for the holy grail of absolute party regularity finally drove him out of the Democratic Party and into the formation of the Progressive Party, on whose ticket he ran for President. In the end, even his own Progressive Party was too irregular for him; he left that one, too. Insisting on party unity all the way, he wound up completely isolated and ineffective, regular only with himself.

I am a Democrat. I have always been a Democrat. I have been elected to public office as a Democrat and I owe a certain obligation to my party. In the exercise of my loyalty to the Democratic Party, I vote for the programs of that party, including those recommended by a Democratic President, as far as my

THE CASE AGAINST REFORM 197

convictions and my conscience will permit me. I will not vote for a piece of legislation I believe to be unconstitutional, no matter who commands it. I will not support a program that, in my judgment, is not in harmony with the best interests of the Nation, no matter who advances it. And the truth of the matter is that even those who prate of party loyalty will themselves desert the party standard on issues close to their hearts.

The doctrine of efficiency leads eventually to a declaration of the majority's right to rule whatever the issue or the consequences. Translating this principle into action, we are told, means amending Rule XXII in the Senate so as to permit a simple majority to gag the minority. The argument between majority rights and minority protection is an ancient one. Others have presented the case against the tyranny of the majority so persuasively that I shall take the liberty of letting them speak for me.

Here, for example, is the late Senator James A. Reed of Missouri:

> Gag rule is the last resort of the legislative scoundrel. Gag rule is the surest device of the rascal who presides over a political convention and proposes to accomplish something which will not bear discussion. Gag rule is the thing that men inexperienced in legislative proceedings always advocate at first, and if they have any sense, nearly always retire from as gracefully as possible after they have seen it in operation. . . .

Here is Senator Robert LaFollette, the elder, of Wisconsin, as great a liberal as ever sat in the Senate:

> Mr. President, believing that I stand for democracy, for the liberties of the people of this country, for the perpetuation of our free institutions, I shall stand while I am a Member of this body against any cloture that denies free and unlimited debate. Sir, the moment that the majority imposes the restriction contained in the pending rule upon this body, that moment you will have dealt a blow to liberty, you will have broken down one of the greatest weapons against wrong and oppression that the Members of this body possess. This Senate is the only place in our system where, no matter what may be the organized power behind any measure to rush its consideration and to compel its adoption, there is a chance to be heard, where there is opportunity to speak at length, and where, if need be, under the Constitution of our country and the rules as they stand today, the constitutional right is reposed in a Member

of this body to halt a Congress or a session on a piece of legislation which may undermine the liberties of the people and be in violation of the Constitution which Senators have sworn to support.

Here is Walter Lippmann:

> In my mind, the proposal to decide highly controversial questions by a vote of no more than one plus one-half of the Senate is not good enough. While the Constitution itself says nothing about the question, it is a fact that the Constitution is by no means devoted to the principle that a simple majority should rule. Treaties and impeachments require two-thirds of all the Senators elected. What is the reason for these exceptions to a simple majority rule? Is it not that what is at stake is of such great moment that it should have the concurrence of more than half of the representatives of the States?
>
> Why should it have this concurrence? Because when controversial matters are decided by a too narrow majority, the prospect of resistance and nullification is increased. To enforce difficult laws, there should be a very large majority which concurs in them.

My own legislative experience convinces me that there must be some one place in our government where someone can say: "Stop! Consider what you are doing. Do not rush into this matter blindly."

I succumbed to that kind of hysteria in 1946 and cast a vote of which I am ashamed to this day. The country was staggering under the impact of a coal mine strike in that year. Coal reserves had dwindled to a point that jeopardized supplies for homes and hospitals. And then the Railroad Brotherhoods threatened to go on strike and paralyze the Nation's transportation system. Responding to a nationwide revulsion to that threat, President Truman sent to Congress a bill that would have given him authority to draft striking railroad men into the Army. The measure was immediately introduced in the House, debated for no more than twenty minutes, and passed by an almost unanimous vote, including mine. Here was the acme of efficiency and speed in an atmosphere of unthinking hysteria.

The bill was rushed over to the Senate where Senators clamored for its immediate consideration and passage. One man objected, Robert A. Taft of Ohio, and under the Senate's rules the matter went over to the next day.

THE CASE AGAINST REFORM

Before the sun rose the next morning, many of us had done a great deal of soul-searching. It dawned on us that we were about to enact a law that violated the prohibitions of the Thirteenth Amendment against involuntary servitude. Only by the grace of one Senator, protected by the rules of the Senate designed to ensure free and full debate, had we been saved from an act of folly. By that next dawn, enough men had recovered from their passions to reconsider and to defeat the bill.

For me, the moral was clear and unmistakable. Yes, Congress is slow and its methods are often cumbersome, and I thank Heaven for it. It is the one body in which every segment of America is represented, where every opinion may be voiced. In a land of such astonishing diversity as our own, diversity of opinion is inevitable. The great function of the Congress is to harmonize that diversity, to compromise the differences, to arrive at a solution with which the Nation as a whole can live in peace. There is no short cut to solutions of that kind. Speed is the enemy of compromise, and compromise is the very essence of our system of government. When you are about to pass a law that will impose restraints on a hundred and ninety-five million people, protracted deliberation is small enough price to ensure a wise and equitable program.

What lies behind the clamor for efficiency, for congressional subservience to the President, for imposing the shackles of party dictatorship on Members of Congress, for abolishing the seniority rule in the appointment of Senate committee chairmen, and for the imposition of gag rule in Senate debate? For the most part, it seems to me, the motive is not one of principle but rather of expedience. What the reformers really have in mind is political advantage, not a worthier or wiser method of governance. Those who cry for "efficiency" and "responsibility" are not so much enamoured of more representative government as they are anxious to justify changes in congressional procedure that will make it easier to pass legislation they favor.

We have considerable evidence on this point. Take, for example, the matter of curbing filibusters. In an earlier day, when political liberals were in the minority in the Senate, they were the most fervent advocates of free debate. I have already cited the words of Senators Reed and LaFollette, two outstanding liberals of the first decades of this century, in passionate opposition to cloture. It can hardly be a coincidence that the American Federation of Labor heartily endorsed uncurbed debate in the Senate during the 1920's, whereas now, when liberals hold a strong position in the Senate, the labor movement just as heartily supports limitations on debate.

The attack upon the seniority system, to take another example, is fundamentally *ad hominem*. It is not the system but some of the men who are made chairmen that rouses the ire of the reformers. And yet a little reflection would make it clear that under a system in which committee chairmen were appointed only if they tagged along with the majority opinion of the party—assuming one could ascertain that opinion in all matters—their friends would be in as much danger as their enemies. Moreover, I wonder how many liberal advocates of stringent party loyalty would mention that position if by some chance conservatives were to dominate the Senate's majority party and dictate the policies to be supported.

Evidently a number of those who formerly proposed all power to the presidency have had second thoughts since the current President adopted a Viet Nam policy not to their liking. More and more we hear pleas for greater congressional initiative in foreign policy from those who once declared foreign policy to be the sole preserve of the Executive Branch and condemned any congressional interference with the President's authority in that area as something akin to treason. All this sounds very much like the teacher applying for a job in Tennessee who was asked: "Are you for or against evolution?" To which he replied: "I can teach it both ways."

Behind the appeals for these "improvements" in our governmental procedures and relationships is the very human but essentially anarchic desire to have it both ways. In effect the reformers say: If the President or the party is on my side, he or it ought to have coercive powers to enforce the policies with which I agree. If, on the other hand, the President or the party is not on my side, they should be shorn of such power. When I am in the majority, all power to the majority; when I am in the minority, unlimited freedom to the minority.

This kind of approach to government makes a mockery of fundamental political principles. It posits a political system with

THE CASE AGAINST REFORM

no rules save expediency. No stable political system can possibly operate on such assumptions. Already the reformers are discovering to their chagrin that there is no guarantee that any governmental agent, to whom power was assigned when he and they were allies, will give up that power when agreement on policy ends. It is far easier to grant a power than to get it back.

The final irony of the situation is that the Congress is in fact a far more efficient institution than we have any right to expect, considering the constitutional framework within which it must operate. The overwhelming proportion of the congressional workload is noncontroversial and this is invariably dispatched with speed and efficiency. It is only on controversial legislation that the Senate slows down to a contemplative walk, and rightly so.

This, after all, was the role intended for the Senate by the founding fathers, to prevent the rash enactment of ill-considered measures. That role has been recognized and valued by every thoughtful student of American Government. Woodrow Wilson went to the heart of the matter when he observed: "The Senate's opportunities for open and unrestricted discussion and its simple, comparatively unencumbered forms of procedure, unquestionably enable it to fulfill with very considerable success its high functions as a chamber of revision."*

Other factors bolster the effective implementation of this great senatorial function. The relatively long term of office and the overlapping tenure of membership give the Senate a permanence and a continuity that is lacking in the House of Representatives and in the presidency. The founding fathers planned it that way to ensure that the Senate might better resist momentary swirls of political passion. Furthermore, the Senate's insulation from those passions is heightened by its representation of the States of the Union as equals rather than proportionately according to population. In short, every constitutional feature of the Senate re-enforces its role as an independent legislative body designed to check the hastiness of the other components of the Federal Government.

It is from this role that the rules, procedures, and practices of the Senate flow as naturally as cool water from a mountain

*Congressional Government, chapter 4.

stream. Only in the Senate is there time for deliberate examination of proposed legislation. Only in the Senate is there an opportunity for all shades of opinion to speak at length and thereby to bring before public opinion the full import of what is proposed.

The conditions of modern senatorial life tend to make the proper implementation of this function ever more difficult. Ideally, a Senator should be in his seat on the floor of the chamber to hear every moment of the debate on all the issues. In fact, this is impossible. We have numerous and often conflicting committee meetings to attend. The Federal Government now touches people's lives at so many points that they are constantly appealing to their elected officials in Washington to intercede for them with the Federal bureaucracy. The average Senator now receives anywhere from 100 to 700 letters a day. Consequently, the burden of office work necessarily cuts into the time he is able to devote to floor attendance.

Under these conditions, protracted debate is often the only way in which a Senator or a group of Senators can catch the attention of their colleagues. And this same situation, by the way, accounts for a good deal of the repetition in debate. Senators often find it necessary to repeat their arguments for the benefit of colleagues who were not present during the main portions of their presentation. It is in this area that the efficiency experts might do the Senate some good.

The country should expect of each Senator that he exercise his best independent judgment. This is not an easy task under the strains of today's legislative pressures. It is made even more difficult by a Senator's often conflicting obligations: to his State, to his party, and to the Nation. But in the last analysis all conflicts must be resolved in favor of that position he believes best for all the people. No one can decide this for him. No party can decide it for him. Only his conscience can guide him. And the Senate will maintain its grandeur so long as it fosters an atmosphere of independence in which each Senator may exercise the freedom to vote and act as his conscience dictates.

The text of this book has been set at The Colonial Press, Clinton, Massachusetts, in 10 point Times Roman with other sizes for introductions and notes. The headings are in Corvinus.

Times Roman was designed by Stanley Morison in this century for the London *Times* and was first used in that newspaper. Its simplicity, directness, and larger letter structure give it its exceptional clarity and legibility.